JUST AN OLD TELEPHONE MAN

"Judge" Pattengill

Table of Contents

DEDICATION

This book is dedicated to all old telephone men and women who took their jobs seriously and worked their hearts out trying to provide the best telephone service in the world. Also, this second edition is dedicated to all those good folks who bought the first edition (See last chapter).

COUNT YOUR BLESSINGS
Count your garden by the flowers
Never by the leaves that fall
Count your days by the golden hours
Don't remember clouds at all
Count your nights by stars, not shadows
Count your life with smiles, not tears
And all throughout your lifetime
Count your age by friends, not years...........Anon.

Photos reprinted with permission from BellSouth (Southern Bell News) and A.T. & T Photo Center.

FOREWARD

I have always been very reluctant to use the term "written by" when referring to the work I did with the first *Just An Old Telephone Man*. Rather, I've simply said that I "put together" some good old telephone stories. I have never claimed to be a writer....just an old telephone man!

The book was published in 2001 and it sold surprisingly well. That encouraged a 2nd Edition. After the initial printing, I have continued to add stories and second thoughts. I have also made many revisions that I should have made before ever releasing it to the printer in the beginning. With time, we all get older and hopefully wiser. Some of the stories in the first edition were a little too descriptive, i.e. certain situations were perhaps too graphic; however the primary reason for a second edition was simply that I had more stories I wanted to tell!

With that, here's the Second Edition of ***Just An Old Telephone Man.*** My most heartfelt thanks go out to all who spend their valuable time with these pages. If they bring a chuckle or a smile, a time remembered, a fond memory of a friend, a longing for the old days, a few moments of nostalgia.....then it's "order completed" and/or "trouble found and repaired!"

The stories and characters contained herein are true except for a little "enhancement" from time to time. Most of the real names and places are disguised. Where they are not, no disparagement is intended.

INTRODUCTION

"I'm the telephone . . . I've come to fix your repairman!"

Back in the good old days when life was simple and people trusted one another and there was a lot less crime, when a woman would let a strange man in her front door just because he was wearing side tools, life as a telephone man was pretty exciting.

Throughout my working days, I observed that "telephone people" have such fun when they're together talking about "on the job" experiences. Volumes have been written about the invention of the telephone and the business in general. There have been movies and TV programs about Alexander Graham Bell and Thomas A. Watson. But, this book is about the day-to-day experiences of a telephone man. Sadly, Ma Bell is gone now and along with her some of the best years of this country's history. And, the telephone business has changed a great deal as well.

These stories are about just plain folks in day to day situations. Lofty credentials, fancy titles, or delusions of power were not a consideration. If you were ever a telephone man or woman, these pages should bring a chuckle or at least a smile. For all other readers, they may make you wish you had been.

For many years, the "telephone man" was trusted and respected possibly more than any other service worker. He was thought of as the cream of the crop as far as service workers go; because, the old companies were particular who they hired. They wanted people for life. They had the reputation of paying well (they really didn't) and being a good solid place to work without fear of layoffs (not always). Their people dressed well and were generally model citizens. They didn't drive Cadillac's or live in mansions, but they could drive a Ford or a Chevy and live in a solid middle class neighborhood.

After a few years with the company, most employees would be accused of having "bell shaped" heads, not referring to appearance, of course, but rather to attitude. The "Bell System" was just that! They had a system of doing things that was standardized for all 23 Bell companies across the United States and Canada too for that matter! It worked so well the Independent Telephone Companies adopted most of the same standards. A craftsman could go to any other town in the country and feel at home with the work and the plant. When there was a major communications breakdown due to hurricanes, tornados, floods or whatever, technicians from around the country would be sent to the scene for the fastest possible restoration. Hand them a map of the town, telephone numbers for dispatch, test desk and assignment and they were just as productive as the hometown guys.

The Bell System was a national treasure that the judges, politicians, and lawyers broke up forever. A world of new technology has come along since the "breakup" and it's debatable whether that would have happened with Ma Bell, but that's another book and another case study altogether. It's a moot point anyway, but until after the old "Bell" people are dead and gone, it will remain a hot topic of conversation among telephone people.

It is important to note that telephone history was not written solely by the old Bell System. It also includes the late and great General Telephone Company, United Telephone, and hundreds of other "Independents" and contractors. They had just as important a role in building the telephone system in this country as did Ma Bell.

"I don't know. I think they ground up coffee beans in it."

Everything that goes around comes around....a familiar old cliché. In recent years, many of the former Bell companies have merged to form very large companies such as Verizon and the new AT&T. What pain, suffering and expense have been experienced in our business! Surely there had to be an easier way to bring about competition. Judge Green and the politicians should have looked to the old Bell Safety Slogan for an appropriate paraphrase, such as: No job is so important and no service so urgent that we cannot take time to properly think the whole thing through.

But this book is about the lighter side of things....

How did the bell ask his girlfriend to get married? He gave her a ring!

An early crew of "Just Old Telephone Men"

"What do you mean you want it on the other side of the street?

CHAPTER 1- COFFEE BREAKS

Since the days of Alexander Graham Bell, telephone men and women have begun their day with a coffee break.

Ummmm...coffee......delicious, nutritious and character-building! “Hey! Where are we going for coffee?" "Oh, we’re all going to Millie's!" "OK! Meet ya' there in ten minutes."

We were supposed to complete our first job before taking a coffee break, but we almost never did. If you wanted to find a telephone man at 8:30 in the morning, you had to know the current coffee shop being used. It's no fun to have coffee alone; it just tastes better with companionship. So, we "congregated" at a prearranged location. You might find as many as fifteen trucks parked around one little coffee shop. Because of the "work first-then coffee" rule, we had to periodically switch coffee shops; but we weren't fooling anyone. The bosses knew where we were most of the time because occasionally the coffee shop telephone would ring with a call from a boss looking for a particular telephone man. Also, sometimes, a couple of bosses (they enjoyed coffee together too) would come into the same coffee shop, have coffee (usually at another table) and be on their way without the first snide remark. Those were the good bosses....some weren't! Occasionally, the bosses would call a bumper meeting and remind us (to put it mildly) that we were not to congregate; so, we would have to abandon the current coffee shop. That same morning, we'd go our separate ways. By the next morning, we had made new plans, agreed on the new coffee shop and were all meeting there as usual! Coffee just tasted better with fellow workers and their stories. By the way, the stories were almost always work experience related thus prompting the writing of this book.

The Phone Business always had more than its share of "characters". A subsequent chapter is devoted to some of these characters; but let me tell you about a few at this point. The "characters" made coffee breaks such great fun. One such character,

Ozzie Coburn, left our table upon seeing an old pickup truck full of homemade lawn furniture pull up. Ozzie was an “old horse trader" from way back and absolutely the best negotiator I've ever known. After leaving our table, someone said, "Better hold on to your wallets!" Sure enough a few minutes later Ozzie returned. "I've got us a deal on that lawn furniture", he said. "If each of us buys a set, he'll let us have it for half price!" Well, even though we had braced ourselves for another one of Ozzie's deals, it didn't sound too bad. So we all got up and went out to look at it. Indeed, it looked pretty good and we all bought a set. Later, we found out that Ozzie got his set free because all the rest of us bought one. He did it to us again!

The current coffee shop was George's Restaurant. A newly hired installer had joined us. He was a nineteen year-old kid who would often go "surfing" before coming to work. He tried to come to work without shoes, but was convinced by his foreman that he really needed them. Anyway, the kid sat down at our table, ordered a Coke and quickly became bored with the adult conversation. After a few minutes, his head fell back against the wall and he was sound asleep. Ben Bland and Mack Stevens, old veteran PBX/Key IRs (Installer/Repairmen), decided to teach him a "rookie" lesson. Since Ben and Mack were riding together, they simply split up. One drove their truck and the other drove the kid's truck to their job site. The rest of us got up quietly and left the kid sleeping at the table. An anonymous phone call to the kid's foreman got him a ride back to the work center along with a few days off without pay. He was fired a few weeks later for coming to work repeatedly without shoes!

And then there was good old Walter Wilson. Poor old Walter was an alcoholic. When the rest of us were having our first cup of coffee, Walter was sneaking a drink from his lunchbox. At quitting time, Walter would sit down at the "meeting room" table to fill out his timesheet. The table would shake so much the rest of us would have to wait until he got up! He got so bad in the latter days that someone had to drive him to the job each day. Once on the job, he would sit down in front of a terminal or cabinet and do whatever wiring or terminating there was to be done....and do it good as or better than anyone else. He was a good telephone man in his younger days, but alcohol had taken its toll. Walter was forced to retire with a disability at age 58. Think about that for a moment! The old Bell System looked after their people. They could have fired Walter with little or no objections from the Union. He clearly had a problem that the Company had to do something about. They chose to handle it in a way that allowed old Walter to leave with his dignity intact. Many years later, I was speaking to an assistant vice president about a concern I had at the time regarding employee morale. He said, "Judge, we really don't care about morale! Those days are gone!" Ah yes, I'm afraid they are. God bless Ma Bell, wherever she is! She cared about morale and old Walter Wilson, and others like him.

Otis Ellison was an IR and one of the nicest guys you'd ever want to meet. He was quiet, unassuming, humble....and a good telephone man. One day, right out of the clear blue sky, he learned that his wife had inherited a small fortune. Seems she was a direct descendant of someone who had founded a major elevator company many years ago. He had died and left her with a great deal of money. The morning Otis learned of his good fortune, we were all congregated at our favorite spot for coffee. His wife came into the little restaurant and broke the good news to Otis as well as to the rest of us. She said, "Now Otis, we're going to celebrate! I want you to order the most expensive thing on the menu and don't worry about the cost." Otis, bless his heart, scanned the menu for a long minute. Then he said to the waitress with complete sincerity, "I'll have fifty dollars worth of them scrambled eggs!"

Scrambled would be a good word to describe Jerry Oshel, a 6-month rookie IR. It was a couple of days before Christmas and workload had slowed a bit in readiness for the holidays. There were only five installers working that day and we had made plans to meet for coffee at 9:30am at the Chatterbox, a popular coffee stop and diner. All but Jerry were right on time. We called dispatch to ask where Jerry was working and two of us jumped in a truck to go find him. We thought we could help him wrap up whatever job he was doing and quickly get back for coffee together. We arrived at his location, went up to the front door and knocked. The customer came to the door in a very obvious state of inebriation. Looking inside we saw Jerry, much in the same state....or even worse! He was so happy to see us and immediately handed us what was left of a bottle of Evan Williams 80 proof Sour Mash

Whiskey. After some amount of conversation, we drove him to his home, drove his truck back to the work center, called dispatch and told them he had gotten sick. No one ever found out and we wrote it off that Jerry's customer had taken unfair advantage of a good, clean-cut kid. The rationalization for an early happy hour with "It must be 5 o'clock somewhere!" took on a whole new meaning for Jerry that day!

Charlie Rice, a veteran IR, was taking his coffee break with several other fellows at a local eatery. After coffee, they all stepped up to the pinball machine for a little entertainment. After about half an hour, the foreman pulled up. He was mad as a wet hen! "I know exactly how long you've been here! Now you all get back to work right now." About the time he had come through the front door, Charlie had won several games on the pinball machine. When the foreman ordered them back to work, Charlie jokingly said, "Come on Joe, I've just won six games on this thing and I'm just getting hot!" The foreman failed to see the humor in his statement. Charlie found out later that Joe had made an entry in his personnel file. Some of the bosses could never lighten up....pity, life it too short for such seriousness.

A good portion of a person's life is given to his/her work. Likewise, a substantial percentage is spent sitting at a table having coffee with a fellow worker. What a great opportunity to get to know that person. One of the beautiful things about working as a telephone man was the camaraderie with fellow workers. I'm sure there were other jobs that offered similar opportunities, but telephone people were special. Of all the good things about working, the people you meet and the friendships you make are the best!

CHAPTER 2 - THE GOOD OLD BELL SYSTEM

There were 23 Bell operating companies in the country. With Divestiture (the breakup of AT&T), the so called Baby Bell companies were created. They were U.S. West, Pactel, Ameritech, Southwestern Bell, Bell Atlantic, BellSouth and Nynex. Later, the names moved ever farther from any connotation of telephone such as Quest, SBC, and Verizon.

<Early Information Desk

Recently, SBC bought AT&T and BellSouth and kept the AT&T name for the whole company. So, once again, the AT&T name is dominant!

I doubt the cost of Divestiture to taxpayers and telephone customers can ever be measured either in terms of dollars or in opportunity costs. Surely if those monies spent had been applied to the already superior telephone service of the old Bell System, we all would be enjoying the benefits today.

Just think! We used to get free repair service on every telephone, every wire or cable, every service. And, free information service to boot!

If there was a problem, we just called Repair Service and it was repaired within two to four hours. Wow! What great service! When we dialed "O", we got an operator who could complete a call from end to end regardless of which companies and how many were involved. When we called the Business Office, we talked with a polite, intelligent person who could handle our complete request, one call one time without punching multiple buttons or wasting a lot of time on hold while listening to tasteless music or boring commercials. When we needed a telephone number, we just called Information (later called Directory Assistance); and it was a free service. We got one bill and we could understand it. Telephone trucks and cars had the local telephone company name on the side, not some "Contractor" company unknown to anyone. If your phone went out, you didn't have to determine where the trouble was yourself before calling repair service. If it turned out to be in the telephone set or inside wire, so what! It was covered! You didn't have to go to the store to buy a telephone. They were provided with the service and were all "Bell System Property". If pre-wiring of a new house or apartment was needed, just call the "Phone Company" and it was done free of charge.

Remember at Divestiture how we were promised that our telephone bills would be reduced? It is definitely true that long distance calls are dirt cheap compared to before, but local service has doubled or more. Now, we must buy our telephones and sometimes pay for repair calls. And, we can't do without our cell phones. Overall, we're spending a lot more, but admittedly we have more services. This is not to say, however, that they wouldn't have been provided in due time by the good old Bell System Companies, perhaps for less money!

The following "opinion" came across my desk about the time of divestiture.

There are in the country two large monopolies. The larger of the two has the following record: The Vietnam War, Watergate, gasoline rationing, runaway inflation and interest rates, and the U.S. Postal Service. The second is responsible for such things as the transistor, the solar cell, lasers, synthetic crystals, high fidelity stereo recording, sound motion pictures, radio astronomy, microwave radio and TV relay systems, electronic telephone switching, the first electronic digital computer, the first communications satellite, and information theory. Guess which one is now going to tell the other how to run the telephone business?

The "GOLDEN BOY" statue (Now in Dallas)

Until recently, this famous bronze statue stood 434 feet atop the AT&T Building at 195 Broadway in New York City. Now, like the rest of us, he has been moved and shuffled around so much, he must be dizzy!

Volumes could be written about Divestiture. It was a miserable experience! Poor old Alexander Graham Bell has surely turned over in his grave many times since Divestiture. With all of the recent mergers, buyouts, and continued talk of such, he probably has a few more times yet to go!

But wait a minute! This book is about the lighter side of the business! So now back to the good stuff!

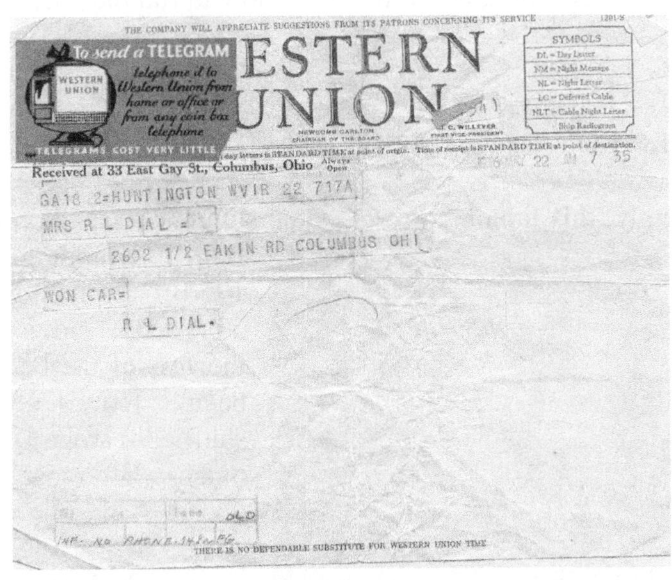
THE COMPANY WILL APPRECIATE SUGGESTIONS FROM ITS PATRONS CONCERNING ITS SERVICE

To send a TELEGRAM telephone it to Western Union from home or office or from any coin box telephone

TELEGRAMS COST VERY LITTLE

WESTERN UNION

NEWCOMB CARLTON, CHAIRMAN OF THE BOARD

C. WILLEVER, FIRST VICE-PRESIDENT

SYMBOLS
DL = Day Letter
NM = Night Message
NL = Night Letter
LC = Deferred Cable
NLT = Cable Night Letter
Ship Radiogram

Time of receipt is STANDARD TIME at point of destination.

Received at 33 East Gay St., Columbus, Ohio Always Open

22 AM 7 35

GA18 2=HUNTINGTON WVIR 22 717A

MRS R L DIAL =

2602 1/2 EAKIN RD COLUMBUS OHI

WON CAR=

R L DIAL.

OLD

INF. NO PHONE

THERE IS NO DEPENDABLE SUBSTITUTE FOR WESTERN UNION TIME

1935 TELEGRAM

Early days "email". Thanks to a dedicated bunch of good telephone people, a better way to communicate was discovered and implemented.

Time out for a “selfie”

CHAPTER 3 - FIRST DAYS ON THE JOB

Joe, a future new hire at the employment office, was alone in the waiting room when he felt the urge to visit the restroom, a door just off the waiting room. Upon returning, he noticed another young man had come in and was patiently waiting his turn as well. Concerned about his competition, Joe turned to him, introduced himself as the personnel manager and apologized saying, "I'm very sorry, but we have just filled our last vacancy. Go on back home now and don't call us, we'll call you."

The old Bell companies didn't hire just anybody right off the street. It was considered such a desirable place to work that they had plenty of applicants and could be very discriminating.

First, the application was highly scrutinized for clarity, punctuation, and neatness. Also, a referral from someone of high standing in the community was very influential in the selection process. A letter from a high school principle was used in my case. A battery of written tests came next, along with a face to face interview. They looked for a level of intellect that would insure success in passing the many technical classes to come later, i.e. Basic Electricity and Basic Electronics to name only two. In fact, the first six months of employment was considered a "probationary period"; and, every new hire was expected to successfully complete the Basic Electricity course within that period.

Before, I couldn't even spell Installer-Repairman. Now, IR one!

Remember seeing that one? It was probably the most common graffiti found in cross-boxes, terminal cabinets or wherever an outside plant telephone man worked (IR was, of course, the abbreviation for Installer-Repairman).

After getting through the hiring process, it was time to report to the job. The installer-repairmen, cable helpers, and linemen would be asked to report to a work center (sometimes called the storeroom in those days). This would generally be a building with parking lot, outdoor storage area for cable, poles, etc., all enclosed in a chain-link fence. Almost everything was painted "Bell System" green trucks, tools, lockers, first aid kits, ladders, signs, doors, floors, desks everything! Imagine the cost of repainting when the new colors of white, blue and ocher were introduced. There were many different types and locations of work centers. Some, for example, were located inside large downtown buildings or perhaps in a telephone central office.

Although our pay didn't begin until 8:00am, our work preparation did. Incidentally, in the mid 1950s, starting pay for an installer was $37.50 per week. Minimum wage was $0.85 per hour or $34 for a 40 hour week. We were expected to arrive at the work center early, pick up our service orders, load our trucks with the proper telephone sets, drop wire, station wire, hardware of all types, and fill our water jugs. Sometimes in winter, we had to put chains on our truck tires for snow and ice conditions. All of this was done prior to 8:00am (on our own time) so we could be ready to pull out of the work center precisely at 8 sharp! This, of course, was a constant point of contention with the union.

The bosses were called Foremen in those days. They were first level managers. They wore dress pants, shirt and tie....yes, a tie! Each had a crew of about 8 to 10 men. At 8 o'clock, they would come out of their office and begin directing traffic exiting the Work Center. To a rookie installer, they were so intimidating that sometimes I would jump in my truck and leave without proper loading just to get away.

A typical first day on the job would generally include meeting the foreman and standing around the work center to observe the morning truck-loading activities and exit described above. Next came some introductions, a brief tour of the work center and a visit to the tool supply area for an issue of tools. An installer's tools would include a side tool pouch and belt, about three screwdrivers of various sizes, long-nose pliers, diagonal (cutting) pliers, gas (large jaw) pliers,

Yankee drill, 216B wrench, installer's test-set (butt-in), and debris brush. Later, for climbing school, the tool issue would include a lineman's belt, safety strap, lineman's hammer, lineman's wrench, lineman's pliers, climbers (hooks or spikes), and ditty (canvas) bag. We didn't know at the time, but our side tools became our ticket to get in almost anywhere.....without question.....including the front door of the customers (called subscribers in those days)!

After the tool issue, it was time for a driving test given generally by your own foreman. A road-marking device with a string reaching to the passenger side of the car would be attached to the front bumper. Upon reaching a speed of 20 mph, the foreman would suddenly pull the string exploding a cartridge marking the road with a spot. At the moment it was heard, the driver would apply the brakes hard enough to cause the wheels to skid and leave tire marks on the road. From this, reaction time as well as actual stopping distance could be measured. A young man with his naturally quick reaction time seldom had any trouble passing the driving test. Afterward, the new installer would receive a "Bell System" driving card, which entitled him to drive company vehicles.

While at this juncture, let's talk trucks. Remember the mid-fifties models? They're classics now! That's a Dodge in the photo below. The drop down door on the side…that's the spare tire! They were all Bell System green of course with the bright gold decals on the driver's door. Some had a metal frame on the rear where cardboard signs were placed periodically. They advertised such things as extension telephones, Princess Sets, long cords, retractable cords, etc. Recall with some of the Bell companies, it was forbidden to get out by the driver's door when it was on the traffic side. We always locked the driver's door, scooted over to the passenger side to exit so we didn't exit into traffic, and locked the door behind us. All storage bins were locked as well when away from the truck. We also curbed the front wheels....toward the curb facing down-hill and away from the curb when facing up hill. The extension ladders were wooden with jagged-steel cleats on the feet that would put a serious dent in the head if you were not careful to duck. They were also very heavy compared to aluminum ladders of today.

Recall the safety slogan on the dashboard or glove-box door?

No Job Is So Important
And No Service Is So Urgent
That We Cannot Take Time
To Perform Our Work Safely.

It was a system-wide slogan that was drilled into all workers from day one!

In 1959, we got our first Volkswagen Micro-Vans. They were a major departure from traditional trucks. We hardly knew how to deal with them. We had to take a short drivers test in order to satisfy the bosses that we could safely operate them. Recall, the brake and clutch pedals were miniature compared to American trucks and required using the toes instead of the entire foot. The driver sat almost forward of the front wheels which made handling quite foreign from anything we had driven before. Then there were the concerns from the Union about buying and driving foreign trucks, especially German. It had not been so long since we were at war with them....and now we were buying and driving their trucks. As it turned out, the American makers came out with their own vans the following year. Vans were cheaper and actually turned out to be ideal. In bad weather, an installer could climb into the back, get his orders out, make up his number cards, add a long cord to a set, make a splice or whatever......and stay dry! And, they were even enjoyable to drive!

In the early Sixties, General Telephone experimented with alternative fuel when they converted each truck from gasoline to propane. A propane gas tank was mounted on top of the truck box with a gas line running to the engine. The conversion was relatively inexpensive and simple....and the propane fuel worked great. But, there was an odor of propane present and we got a lot of comments. “Are you cooking something in that thing?” “Where do you keep your BBQ grill?” “Is that thing about to explode?”

The original purpose was not to save gasoline costs; gasoline was cheap in those days. The chief reason was to save maintenance costs. Converting liquid gasoline into a gas by the carburetor was a major source of problems. Carburetors would gum up and clog up requiring trips to the garage. The propane required no such conversion and was much cleaner burning. I’m not sure what the experiment proved, but it was not continued probably because gasoline was so cheap. These days with higher gasoline prices, I wonder why we aren’t seeing more of that type of conversion.

Meanwhile, let’s get back to those first days on the job. My first day included another unforgettable event. My foreman asked where I lived and we actually drove by my home to have a look. He wanted to get to know not only my work ethic, but also something about my home life. Years later, I learned he had documented the visit with a statement to the effect, "He appears to have had a very happy childhood and happy home". These days, they check for criminal record and do drug tests. Who cares about a happy childhood and home life?

At some point during those first few days, all new employees were introduced to the most basic phone company rule book...The Three Cs. Most firings were a result of someone ignoring and violating one or more of the Three C's. Any telephone employee can tell you what the C's stand for...Cash, Copper, and C--- (several words starting with C that refer to the female anatomy or companionship of one type or another). The companies were very tolerant of many things, but very intolerant of violations relating to the Three Cs. There was so much emphasis on them that if caught in violation, there were very few excuses to justify. This, of course, meant absolutely no taking of cash and/or copper. The other "C" commonly referred to those who got inappropriately involved with the opposite sex (certainly customers, but also employees) while on the job. Throughout my years, there were always periodic situations when someone failed to heed the "Three C's" warnings and ended an otherwise good career. And, it was across all positions from entry-level craft up through vice presidential level.

Day two on the job began at the work center with everyone except the new hires scurrying around getting their trucks loaded and pulling out under the boss's direction precisely at 8 o'clock. The rookies would either ride with someone for a while or maybe work left-ins. In the latter case, they were assigned a truck and handed a stack of "left-ins". A "left in" is a telephone which had been previously disconnected, but not removed. For example, if someone moved out of a house before the telephone was removed, then the service would be disconnected at the terminal (on the pole or in a terminal closet) and if access to the house could not be gained, the telephone would be "left in" place. Since the old Bell System owned all telephones and reused them repeatedly, it was important to keep track of them and to keep going back until access could be gained and the telephone removed. Imagine the records headaches that entailed.

So, working "left-ins" was simply an exercise in locating a street address, driving to it and finding and removing the non-working telephone set. This was a good way to begin a new installer. It provided some practice with driving a company truck, learning to use a street map and finding addresses, personal skills in meeting with people, and limited training with tools, telephone sets and connecting blocks. A new installer might work "left-ins" for a couple of weeks before progressing to anything more demanding.

My first day of "left-ins" resulted not only in gaining the above-mentioned experience, but also it introduced me to an early morning phenomenon. I learned a woman would let me in her door simply because I was wearing side tools and answered "Telephone Man" to the question, "Who's there?" I'll have much more to say about that in a later chapter.

Another second day activity might include climbing school. Many work centers had a few poles set up, usually near the "pole yard", for just such a purpose. Climbing required a lot of practice and it was hazardous to say the least. The instructor would always warn his students to push away from the pole if your hooks ever "cut out". Easy to say! The natural inclination is to grab the pole and hold on for dear life, the exact wrong thing to do! In the first place, you can't hold on to the pole without sliding down. In the second place, every splinter in the pole will wind up embedded in your arms, legs, chest, neck and other unmentionable places. This is, of course, the last thing a climber wants because all of the pain and carnage is compounded by the creosote in the splinters. In addition to the threat of cutting out, it was also possible to seriously injure yourself with the hooks. Each hook had a gaff (sharp spike) which had to be super hard and sharp to penetrate the poles. That gaff could also penetrate a leg or foot. I doubt there are very many climbers who have not gaffed themselves at one time or another, this old climber included!

The second week on the new job might include some "cutover" work. The term "cut-over" refers to several different types of work operations. Usually it is thought of as converting service from one type of office to another, i.e. when we transferred service from one type of switching equipment to a newer type of switching equipment. This was done frequently in faster growing areas where old offices would reach capacity and new ones were added. This type of cutover generally involved large numbers of subscriber lines (customers).

Cutover also referred to the transfer of service from one distribution facility to another, i.e. from cross-arms and open wire to new cable. We used to speak often of "Universal Service", a term referring to a nationwide goal of making telephone service available to every household throughout the country. Recall, telephone service was not readily available to many rural areas until well into the 1950s.

Universal service happened in gradual steps of replacing open wire (iron or copper wire on cross-arms) with cable, or simply placing new cable to areas where telephone service had never been available. Once this was done, it became the job of the cutover crews to transfer the service drops from the old wire to the new cable. In areas where service was provided for the first time, installation crews would go door to door, first selling then installing the necessary wiring and the telephone set. There will be more about cutover in a later chapter.

Those first few days at the work center were so very exciting! There were the trucks (all shapes and sizes), cable reels, poles, men running around doing things, foremen shouting orders, etc. The linemen always wore long sleeve shirts (usually flannel), jeans and climber's boots (the ones that had the extra leather strap up the inner-side where the metal climbers rubbed against). The cable splicers sometimes wore coveralls and always had their splicer's scissors in a leather holster attached to their belt. Installers/repairmen were able to dress in perhaps more normal street clothes since they regularly worked inside homes and businesses.

Johnny Carson once said he was so naive as a kid that when he went out behind the barn, he didn't know what to do! That was me as well. As a rookie, it quickly became obvious that I was more in the way than anything else. And, it was like someone had hung a "New Hire" sign on my back. Some would extend a warm welcome, but there were a few who delighted in having fun with the new kid.

"Hey son, hand me that fish tape!" "Huh! What's a fish tape?" Of course, that kind of request would always be given when several of the older men were there to witness and have their laughs. There were a blue million new things to learn. "Hey boy, grab the end of that pole and help me move it over a few feet!" Was I really supposed to be able to do that? A typical pole weighs several hundred pounds which was far more than two men can carry. I didn't know that! So, he would walk over, grab one end and look at me like he expected me to do the same, and, being a rookie, I would! Then the laughs came!

The initial tool issue included a "dial" screwdriver. It's a small tool used for very small screws and adjustments such as were required on rotary dials. The storeroom guys would hand you that one and say, "Oh, this one is for picking door locks. If there is no one home, use this to pick the lock and go on in". In those days, a telephone man had almost unquestioned access to about anywhere there was a telephone. Remember, all equipment belonged to the company. Customer owned equipment did not exist! So, if it was telephone equipment, it belonged to the company; therefore, we must have a right to go in to work on it. Wrong! But it seemed logical at the time and the lock picking screwdriver made sense to a rookie.

All trucks carried a canvas bag containing a pair of leather gloves, rubber gloves and thin glove liners. The rubber gloves were for use when high voltage was present or even suspected. Their ability to protect against high voltages was directly related to the integrity of the rubber. If the gloves had been penetrated and thus had leaks, they could no longer protect completely against the high voltages. As a part of the routine inspections, gloves were tested for leaks. There was a standard procedure for doing this which involved folding over the top of the glove and spinning around until the trapped air would create pressure in the hand and finger area of the glove. A keen ear could detect an air leak much like listening for a leak in a bicycle inner-tube. I had been shown this procedure once in the work center. One day in those first few weeks, I was visited on the job by my foreman. He asked me to test my rubber gloves. I promptly grabbed the bag, pulled out the first glove and proceeded to try to blow it up like you blow up a balloon. I remembered the concept, but forgot the method. How embarrassing! Good grief, there were so many of those humiliating moments while we all tried to get up to speed in our training. Some of the foremen helped without laughing at us.....some did not!

So, the first six months were spent trying to figure out the good advice from the bad. No harm was meant by anyone. It was just fun to show the rookies how much they had to learn. It was a way to bring them into the "family". It helped them get over any cockiness they might have brought in with them. It was for their own good so the older guys said! Also during the first six months, all new people were sent to a company school for initial training. If the foremen were good at their on the job training, by the time the formal school was scheduled the training was almost academic. At some point in the Sixties, the companies introduced training schools for Basic Electricity and Basic Electronics for the plant people. These schools proved to be very difficult for some of the older workers as they required a working knowledge of Algebra, Trig and Calculus.

I imagine there is quite a period of adjustment for a new hire to begin work on any job. Looking back on the whole experience, it was very unpleasant at times, but also fun and exciting. Most made the cut without too much difficulty, but some didn't. I remember a new hire that came to work wearing a baseball cap with "OPS" on the front. He was fresh out of the military, still wearing his service cap. The older men began calling him "Oops"! This bothered him so much that he eventually resigned!

As time on the job went along, an installer's experience began to show. For example, diagonal pliers, (called Dikes) were to an installer as a scalpel is to a surgeon. Terminating JK or cable on a connecting block by an experienced IR could be a fascinating performance to the on-looker. There was no need for a wire stripper, in fact, that was a laughable tool. We carried them, but only for drop wire. Diagonals could remove the jacket with one motion and each wire could be stripped and terminated in a split second! An experienced installer could mesmerize an audience with his amazing dexterity and expertise!

The strength of youth was another definite advantage. Brute strength can sometimes be the difference between completing a job or not. Naturally, strength is essential for lineman's work. A weakling simply cannot raise a cross arm loaded with insulators! Strength was important to the installer-repairman as well. Toll repair for example required carrying tools, wire, test sets, etc sometimes for several miles. Even installation sometimes required crawling around under houses or in attics.....not an easy or very pleasant thing to do. The installer was on the job by himself, i.e. anything the job required was done alone. Extra trips back to the truck for something forgotten was not only discouraged, but also adversely reflected in low work units. Worse, an extra trip or two up and down a pole for a tool, an attachment, or a dropped tool was ever so frustrating! At the end of a hot day, those young strong guys were still talking about what they were going to do during the evening hours. The older ones were looking forward to a cold beer and a recliner! Like the words of the country song by the group, Alabama, we worked our forty hour week just to pass it on down the line. At Divestiture, our customers, for whom we worked our hearts out trying to give them the best service possible, seemingly couldn't have cared less!

THE LINEMAN

This is the famous Norman Rockwell illustration of a telephone lineman passing a cable lasher from one side of a pole to the other. They don't do much to that anymore, huh!

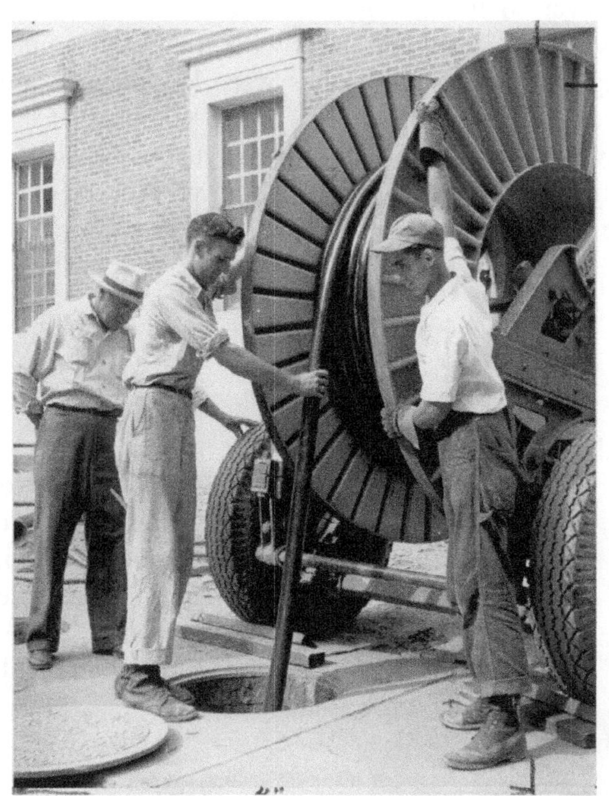

"Let's get those safety glasses on, boys".

CHAPTER 4 - A TYPICAL WORK DAY

<Anything done next will definitely be WRONG!

Oh no! Is that the alarm clock already? Is that all there is to a night's sleep? Oh well! It's out of bed, get dressed, grab a cup of coffee and head out to work. Upon arrival, the work center is already bustling with activity. The Linemen and Splicer's often reported earlier than the Installation-Repair group. It helped to relieve some of the congestion of people at the work center and since they did not work in people's homes, they could get an earlier start. It also allowed them to beat a little of the heat.

So, you make your way toward the Installation-Repair end of the work center. You find your mailbox and pull out the day's stack of orders. Then you flip through the addresses on the orders to find out which part of town you'll be working in. Or, there were some who worked in large cities and permanently assigned to one building.

Let's talk orders for a minute. Orders had various designations, but the most common were N, T&F, C, M, and O. N orders (formerly "I" orders) were for new service. T&F were for customers moving to a new address from their former one. C orders were for change of service, such as changing from party line service to private line. O, or out orders, were for disconnect of service. M orders were for moves, i.e. an inside move of a telephone set. There were others as well, such as R orders used to change records for one reason or another.

So, you glance through your stack of orders. You see a couple of N orders in a new sub-division. Oh no! Those will be brand new installs with new drop, protector....the works! But, then you have several N's, T's & F's and C's in one apartment building. Those will be easy. It shouldn't be any trouble to make work units today!

Work units? Well, it was a weighting system according to type of work operation for measuring efficiency. And, it wasn't always very fair. It could be degrading as well because everyone's results were posted on a bulletin board for all to see. Same with sales of extension phones, color sets, long cords and the like! Whose idea was that? We weren't salesmen, we were telephone installers! We did it just the same! When working in a rural area, many N and T orders were new installs. It was sometimes very difficult to make work units when having to place new drop wire, protector, ground and inside wire. Conversely, it was very easy when working in an urban area. There you might have ten orders in one apartment building. You could go to the terminal cabinet and run all required cross-connects on one trip. Then you could grab all your sets, make up all the number cards, grab enough directories and work all ten orders almost simultaneously.

Now that your orders are in hand, you walk to your truck to check your set inventory. In some areas, the storeroom personnel would load the trucks each night. In others, it was up to the IR to determine what he would need for the day and get the supplies from the storeroom. Other than telephone sets, you would need a supply of drop wire, inside or station wire (JK), directories, drive hooks, drive rings, protectors, ground wire, ground straps, ground clamps, staples, connecting blocks, C clamps, drop wire clamps, S clamps, etc, etc, etc. Our trucks were most always well supplied, and it was up to each person to make sure it stayed that way.

At this point, it is worth noting that on mornings when a heavy snow came down shortly before 8 o'clock, we were asked to put on our tire-chains. It was not in our job description and often a bone of contention with the union, but we did a lot of things not within our job description. In short, we did what we needed to do to get the job done. Service was king...the ultimate goal....our main purpose for being!

Let's see......what's the address on that first order? Hopefully, it's in the general direction of the coffee shop. After coffee, you pull up to your first job, curb your wheels and strap on your side tools. You have your order-clip in hand along with the required set and directory. By that time, it's almost nine o'clock. The housewife comes to the door and cracks it only about an inch. You say the magic words….."Telephone Man"! The cute little housewife sees your side tools, knows you are a telephone man and she opens the door with no further questions asked. She is still in her housecoat, but thinks nothing of letting the most trusted service worker in her front door. After learning where she wants her telephone installed, you put your buzzer on the nearest connecting block and head outside to the protector. After removing the cover and checking to see if the buzzer's tone is leaving on the drop wire toward the pole, you head back to the truck to get your climbing gear on. You take your hooks in hand (recall, you didn't walk with hooks on) and head for the alley out back. You find your pole, get your hooks on (don't forget to remove the yellow protectors) climb up and begin your search for the drop with the buzzer tone. If you're lucky, you might find a drop with a little clear plastic tube on the end and a white tag inside with your address on it. You clip one of your installer's test set clips on a ground (cable, terminal or power ground) and the other clip to your drop. Hopefully, your buzzer tone is coming in loud and clear. Next, open up the terminal lid. Watch out for those roaches, wasps and scorpions! You clip on to a pair of bind posts with your test set, flip the monitor/talk switch and get dial tone. Then dial up your telephone number and hope to hear the audible ring. If so, it means the frame has probably worked their portion of the order and you should have your number coming to you on the assigned cable pair. If not, you will have to call and ask that they get your order worked ASAP. You hear the audible ring....good. Then you grab your trusty 216-B tool and "run the terminal" while listening and watching for the binding posts that trip the ring when shorted. There were other more correct ways to find your pair, but none quicker. Recall, in those early days, there were very few private lines and special services and you didn't worry so much about interrupting a service. In fact, they were almost non-existent in residential areas. Running the terminal would only cause a crack in the ear of anyone talking on the line.....so, not to worry! After finding your pair, you connect the drop wire and climb back down the pole. We haven't talked about dogs at this point. If there was a mean dog anywhere in the neighborhood, it would be at the base of my pole waiting to get a taste of my leg! Dogs were quite a challenge to a telephone installer so I've devoted a later chapter to the subject.

Another challenge to the installer was the infamous SWT. Remember them? It was a Service Wire Transfer or otherwise known as a throw, a swat or a cut. It referred to the practice of moving an existing subscriber from one pair to another so as to make room for the new subscriber service on your order. Commonly, it meant going to an address somewhat close to your order, climbing the terminal pole, calling the frame, and moving the drop from one pair to another. If you were so unfortunate, it could mean finding the "throw to" pair in the wad of cable pairs in a ready access terminal......what a mess! Ready Access was invented by a very smart engineer who had never worked installation in his life! The idea of having access to every pair in the cable at every terminal must have seemed like the ultimate solution to efficient cable fill. In reality, it was a repairman's nightmare as well as the installer's. After even a small amount of work at the terminal, the order (or disorder) of the cable pairs invariably got so bad that any movement within the terminal would surely cause other (man-made) troubles.

"I rather hesitated to bother you. The woman next door said you probably couldn't afford one."

Well, back to our service order. Upon getting the line to the house, it was common practice to thoroughly check the protector, the fuses and/or carbons, the ground wire and the terminal-post connections. We carried a "tool brush" with a wooden handle to brush out the spider webs, wasp nests and dirt that may have accumulated inside the protector. When satisfied the outside wiring was OK, then it was into the house to install the telephone. Until the late Fifties and into the Sixties, most households had only one telephone. Extensions were not uncommon necessarily, but they did cost an extra $1.50 per month and most people did not want the added expense. Of course, we were expected to try to sell them along with all the other add-ons such as long (mounting) cords, retractable (handset) cords, color sets, Princess Sets, etc. The choice of black telephone sets varied with the current supply from Western Electric. The best one was a new 500 (desk set), but there were also refurbished 500s, 5302s (an old 300 retrofitted to look something like a 500) and even 300s. Wall sets were also of the 500 and 300 types designated as 554s and 354s respectively.

After connecting the mounting cord with its three spade-clipped red, green and yellow leads under the screws of the connecting block, hopefully you could hear dial tone with the handset. If it was a private (individual or single) line, there was no concern about which side of the line was tip or ring, and a ground was not required. The red lead was typically terminated under the Line One (L1) screw of the connecting block. And, the green and yellow leads were both terminated on the L2 side. A ring-back code could be dialed to make sure the ringer was working properly and to check the adjustment for volume. The number card was placed inside the round number card holder and placed back on the front of the finger wheel. With that, the dutiful installer would call Dispatch, verify all equipment on the premises, sign off (or pass) the order and confirm his next destination. He would then thank the housewife and be on his way to the next order.

Sometimes during a typical day, Dispatch would add an order to the day's workload. It might be one that fell through the crack for one reason or another. Sometimes it would be a DNP (Disconnect for Non-Payment). I always hated those orders. Invariably, it was a family down on their luck; and, losing their telephone was the last thing they needed. One was particularly distasteful that I still remember after many years. It involved someone whom I knew personally. I'll get back to that story in a subsequent chapter.

After working a few orders, lunchtime would roll around. Many carried their lunch and ate in their trucks while parked in a shady spot. Others bought lunch at the nearest restaurant and some drove back into the work center. Lunch at the work center was always a treat due to the conversation with fellow IRs. That's where many of these stories came from! On many days, there would be a game of cards...often Hearts. I thought I was an expert Hearts player until playing with the lunch-crowd at the work center. The term "Cut-throat" Hearts took on a whole new meaning. It could be downright humbling!

Well, it's back to work! Next order is for new service way out in the sticks. The cable assignment is out of the last terminal on the cable. The big question is just how far the house is from the terminal.....not a pleasant question to ponder! After a nice drive with arm out the window, you arrive at the terminal pole. Now you start your search for the actual house. There are no house numbers, just a Rural Route Box Number. There is little hope of finding it without asking someone who lives nearby. So you stop the truck at a house you know has been occupied by one family for many years. Directly (as they say in country), the owner comes walking around the side of the house. She is red-faced from the sun and is holding her apron in the form a basket which is full of freshly-picked tomatoes. Naturally, she knows the new people on your order. She knows everything that goes on in her neck of the woods. You learn the new folks are the fifth gravel drive down the road on the left. She offers you a few tomatoes which are readily accepted and immensely appreciated.

The fifth drive on the left just happens to be a new house, never had a telephone and nine spans from the terminal. Oh No! You look up at the pole line which already has about 10 drops spanning the poles. You recall turning this area into the Engineering Department for new cable the last time you had an order here. Way to go Engineers! Thanks for ignoring my request. Now I've got to string another nine spans of drop. Oh well, might as well get to it. You set your drop wire reel down at the pole serving the house. Then you get your hooks on, grab some drop wire clamps, grab the end of the wire and begin walking toward the terminal pole. You hope there is enough wire on the reel to make it all the way to the terminal. Having to make a stagger-splice would take an extra 10 minutes. You have your side tools on (as always), but you leave your big, heavy body belt and safety strap in the truck. You're an old experienced climber and you know it's just a quick trip up each pole, place a couple of clamps on the wire, hang them on an existing drive hook and back down. The technique requires wrapping one leg around the pole at working level so as to free your hands. We were strong as horses in those days and we could work in that somewhat awkward position for quite a spell if need be. A safety inspection would be disastrous at that point, but they seldom happened that far out in the country. With experience, you knew what you could get away with and what you couldn't! Even though you didn't use your body belt, you knew to keep your protectors on your hooks while walking between poles. A gaff injury was the last thing anyone wanted.

Whew! What a job, but you got it done and are now making that long awaited trip back into town with the arm out the window. This time, you hold your arm a little farther out so the wind comes in your shirt sleeve and helps dry your sweat-soaked shirt!

Next is a C Order to change the service from party line to single line......an easy job! You're ready for an easy one after the last one. You knock on the door and verify with the lady customer what you're about to do. She tells you about the side gate that she will unlock so you can get back to the pole. You won't need hooks this time because the pole is stepped. So, with body belt on, you head back through the gate and toward the pole. Once in the back yard, you notice a young girl in bathing suit lying on a blanket sun bathing. She must be the daughter, but WOW....is she a knockout! You say hello and climb up to your ringside seat at the top of the terminal pole. You lean back in your body belt, get situated and dial up the frame on your test set. You're in no hurry....the scenery is beautiful! Shucks! This time they answer almost immediately and are working your order by the time you get off the pole.....just my luck!

Well, let's call it a day! You've made your work units....time to go in. Upon getting back to the work center, you grab your bag of tomatoes from the front seat and your orders (now wrinkled, dirty and still damp from sweat) and head for the work room to fill out your timesheet. The big fan on a stand feels good.....air conditioning is still several years away. On the other end of the table is good old Walter Wilson. He's had a rough day without nearly enough booze to get him through. He shakes the table as he struggles to make out his timesheet. No one minds though. In spite of his problem, he's a good telephone man and has paid his dues!

It's time to head home. The end of the work day finally rolled around. And what was the best part about it? You left it there until 8 o'clock the next morning! No brief case, no working at home after hours, no more phone calls for the day.....just sweet relaxation with your wife, kids and the dog.

"Come on Joe! I know you love your job, but you've got to go home sometime!"

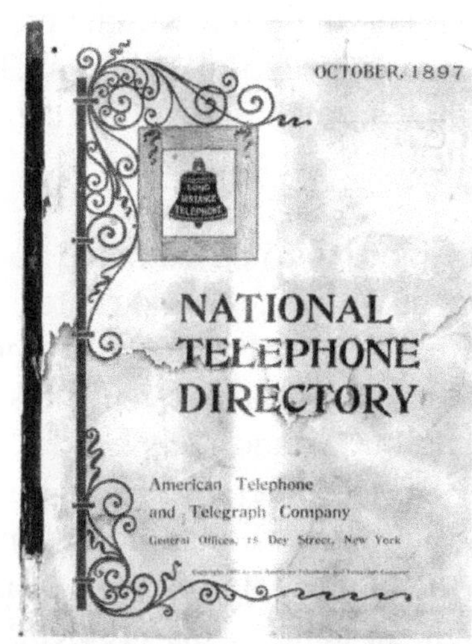

CHAPTER 5 – CHARACTERS

Woodrow Smith would have married Ma Bell if he could have. Woodrow was my first boss and fit the title of Mr. Telephone Company better than anyone I ever knew. He was small in stature, but a giant in leadership. As a first level Installation Foreman, his job was to make sure telephones were installed to quality standards of the Bell System. Quantity and safety were the other two buzzwords of the day that every self-respecting telephone man took to bed with him each night. Woodrow made sure of that! "How are you liking it?" Woodrow would say as a greeting to the new installers. A negative reply was never given even if felt. He was so enthusiastic about his job and the telephone business; it couldn't help but rub off on the new employees.

It almost goes without saying that Woodrow did everything by the book (The Bell System Practices or BSPs). One incident called for a solution not in the book and Woody came through. A rookie installer had mistakenly drilled up from the basement instead of down from the main floor into the basement. The drill bit came out on in the middle of the beautiful wood floor. The customer had not seen it, but surely would on the first trip by. All installation trucks were equipped with drawers and bins filled with all sorts of things for the job, but not new flooring. Frantically, the installer called Woody. The old pole mounted terminals in those days had holes in the back which were there to accommodate drop wires. When a drop wire was removed, it left the hole unoccupied and was an invitation for wasps, scorpions, etc. to enter and make a home. To combat this, the trucks carried small round corks with which to plug the holes. Well, Woody calmly told the rookie installer to plug the hole in the flooring with a round cork and then take some iodine from his first-aid kit and stain the cork to match the oak floor. The customer never knew of the mishap or the subsequent repair.

Another character was Bill McQuinn. He was a district level with an "independent" company who once hired me...back in my younger days. My first encounter with him came when I went in for the initial interview. I had already completed the job application and was at the second step in the hiring process. Bill McQuinn had a gorgeous secretary who had an equally nice figure. When I arrived, she went into Bill's office to announce my presence. Just as she was about to turn around and walk back to her desk, Bill grabbed her around the hips and pulled her up against him. Then she bent over and kissed him while he continued to pat her behind. All of this was done while they both knew full well that I could see right through the doorway and witness the whole thing. As a young installer who respected upper level managers (almost feared them), this was outside my frame of reference. I had my interview a few minutes later and got the job, but I never had any respect for him after that. Fortunately, I never had to deal with him again, but always wondered why a man in his position would do such a thing. And, it was in violation of the "Three Cs" explained in a previous chapter.

Then there was Otis (Ot) Sampson. "Ot" worked his eight hours, i.e. about four for Ma Bell and four to satisfy his social calendar. He was indeed a ladies' man and got most of his dates on the job. Ot was on a trouble call once when he went to the building terminal to call the test desk. While waiting his turn with the test deskman, he began periodically listening in on a conversation on the next binding post. The conversation was between two pimps who were discussing their current rosters of "ladies of the evening". When the test deskman got around to Ot, he was asked if he had found his trouble yet. Ot replied, "No, but I got some doggone good leads."

Ray Pittman had something other than driving on his mind as he made his way to the first order of the day. He must have been looking around for something in the seat or glove box and it cause him to weave as he drove down the road. Low and behold, a "black and white" with blue lights flashing pulled in behind him. Ray pulled over wondering what the cop wanted. After all, he was driving a green telephone truck.....not an emergency vehicle, but a rather official service vehicle of some importance at least in Ray's mind. The cop asked Ray if he was OK. Ray said, "Of course, why?" The cop said, "Well, you were weaving back and forth within the lane!" Ray said, "But I was looking for the address on my service order!" Well, the cop didn't buy it and said, "I'm going to have to give you a 204". Ray said, "Wait a minute! What's a 204?" "Oh", the cop said, "It's just the number of the ticket we give for weaving." Old Ray was livid by this time and he said, “Well old buddy, you might as well make it a 408 ‘cause I’ll be coming right back through here tomorrow!”

The phone business had to have been one of the worst companies (aside from the government) about promoting people to their level of incompetence. The traditional upward mobility with a telephone career began at the entry-level craftsman through journeyman level and eventually to a management position, at least for some. It didn't seem to matter whether there was any managerial ability or not. If a person was a good craftsman, then the company often figured that person would make a good manager....not necessarily so!

There were many examples of the above, but one of the best was Ed Reese. Ed couldn't make a decision if his life depended on it. If there was ever a "yes man", Ed was it. If his boss ever stopped suddenly, Ed would run right into him. It was my misfortune to work for Ed for a short time. According to Bell System tradition, work groups and foremen were constantly changing, supposedly for cross training. It also provided much needed relief from bosses like Ed. On my last day before transferring from one Bell Company to another, Ed stayed with me the entire day. It was raining cats and dogs and he gave me a dirty cutover job in a back alley and stayed with me to make sure I put in a full day's work. I didn't mind the work, it was just another day to me, but it was humiliating that an incompetent “boss's whipping boy” could stand over me and supervise me. There were others like him throughout my working career, but he was the worst! That incident convinced me to go back to school and strive for a higher job.

Thank goodness, there were many more really great folks than there were bad ones...such as Jack Rooper. Jack was a fellow installer who taught me more about doing quality work than any foreman ever did. I remember once, after working through all my orders, I went over to one of Jack's jobs where he was doing a new installation. It was a very large new house and Jack was up in the attic running wire when I arrived. I found his ladder and climbed up to see what I could do to help. There was Jack meticulously wiring a terminal block on the side of a two-by-six roof truss. In a few days, the builders would have the sheetrock installed and the attic would be sealed. Unless there was trouble of some kind, the terminal that Jack was wiring would never again be seen by a human being. No matter to Jack! He carefully arranged each station wire and conductor so that they came into the block exactly like every other one. Red, green, yellow, black, all nice and neatly terminated just like it was pictured in the BSP's. Jack was like that. To the telephone service, it didn't really matter that the wires were in such perfect order....but it did to Jack...and it did to me too after seeing his example.

Another character was Jim Bowen. I had the good fortune of working an "out of town" assignment with Jim, which gave me a chance to get to know him. He was not only a fine individual, but also a very good telephone man. He was very active with the union (CWA - Communications Workers of America) and always had something to say at the meetings. I remember one meeting got off to a rousing start with Jim immediately taking the floor. After some discussion which few seemed to understand, Jim was heckled with a few shouts of "Get to the point, Jim!"

"After considering all of the facts in the matter presently on the floor and before us tonight" he would say in his most oratorical manner, "I am of the opinion that a grievance is indeed justified. Therefore, after deep soul searching and serious contemplation, I move that we go forward with our right to file a grievance against this obviously premeditated act of harassment", Jim continued. "But Jim, what did the foreman do or say to you?" someone asked. "Well", Jim said, "When I came to work yesterday morning, he accused me of deliberately holding my bladder until 8 o'clock so I could go to the restroom on company time!"

Another "Jim" story comes to mind. Jim was one of the oldest IRs in the group. I was never sure why he had been passed over at promotion time, maybe due to his dedication to union activities. Jim was a rather serious type who never participated in any of the "horse play" that was common with the others. He would always have some remark about the "children" engaging in such adolescent games. His serious approach to work got such attention that the others (especially the older guys) delighted in doing things to interfere with his routine. If he would place something on top of his truck for loading later, someone would invariably hide it. When he got in his truck to pull out, someone would block him in. Once, he found grease all over his steering wheel. Another time, he was having trouble pulling out only to discover someone had put chocks in front of his wheels. And, they were always hiding his lunchbox, which would infuriate him.

Jim's habit of heading to the restroom at about 8 o'clock every morning before leaving the work center just invited the others to kid him about it. One particular morning, he followed his routine and headed to the restroom. All three stalls were in use. Jim paced back and forth in the outside hallway periodically checking the stalls for a vacancy. After a lengthy wait and bulging eyeballs, Jim learned the guys had placed empty boots in each of the three stalls. It was not funny at least to Jim. Everyone else died laughing!

Mack Stevens also makes the "character" list. I was working with Mack (as his helper) on a "1A key" job. We introduced ourselves to the customer, some kind of small manufacturing business I believe. The service order called for six telephone sets. Mack asked the customer where the equipment room was located and proceeded to explain how we had to mount an equipment cabinet and power supply on the wall near the drop entrance. After looking at the room with the customer, Mack then asked where he wanted the telephone sets. At that point, the customer seemed as though he had wasted enough time with us and told us to put them anywhere we thought appropriate and he left the building, got in his car and was gone! Mack decided he would make it a short day! We ran one ten-foot piece of cable to the room adjacent to the equipment room and installed all six sets right there! (I don't recall hearing anything further from the customer!)

Art Hoffman was another "character". We attended Basic Electricity School together. The company reserved rooms for us at an old hotel in downtown near the central office, where the school was held. Of course, every evening after dinner, we would hit the "watering holes" until time to go to bed. One evening, Art had a few too many. I left him heading for his room and I went into mine. A few minutes later, I heard someone fumbling with the lock on the door. I opened it only to find Art trying to get his key into my door. After explaining that he was at my room by mistake, I sent him on his way and went to bed. After a while, I heard the same fumbling at the door. Sure enough, it was Art trying to get into my room again. "Art", I said, "You have the wrong room again, this is my room". He said, "Oh, OK" and left again. Now I'm back in bed and the whole thing is repeating itself again with Art fumbling at the door once more! Again, I opened the door to find him with key in hand trying to hit the keyhole once more. "Art, this is not your room, this is my room!" I said with obvious irritation! With greatly slurred speech, Art said "Well dog-gone! You've got every room in the hotel!"

It was commonplace to come into the work center at lunchtime when we were working close by. However, lunch was so much fun with a bunch of the guys telling their stories, that many times guys would drive far more miles than they should just to eat there. One day, Calvin Moore was telling of working somewhere out in the country. He had been installing a new service in a farmhouse. All morning, he had smelled some awful odor coming from the kitchen. Calvin said, “Would you believe the lady was cooking ‘chitlins and hog jowls’ in the same pot!” He said, “It was the only time I’ve ever seen flies trying to get out of the house!"

Driving a long distance just to have lunch in the work center actually came in second place to driving a long distance to get a paycheck cashed. Back in the days before "direct deposit", payday meant a sure stop at the bank to get your check cashed. For many, it also meant money for lunch that day. Occasionally, the foremen would warn us all in a meeting that we were not to drive out of the way to the bank. One particular recollection of an "out of the way" trip occurred when Frank Mondale, an IR, drove twenty two miles from his work location in the country to an in-town bank and back to his work location on his lunch hour (more or less). Alas, he was caught and sent home for a day without pay. Poor old Frank just stretched it a bit too far!

I was installing a new service in a community we facetiously called Cowtown. The foremen rarely made it to Cowtown because it was a 15-mile drive from the work center. This day, however, my foreman, Tom Nordstrom, came by to check on me. I was running "JK" wire around a baseboard and I apparently wasn't putting in quite enough staples to suit old Tom. After he suggested I put more in, he said, "Judge, it's kind of like the old maid said about kissing. You just can't hardly overdo it!"

No one ever loved to "act a fool" any more than Harry Webster. He had very few serious moments. Once, I was asked to go by and help him with installing a new drop wire (the wire from the pole to the building). Harry was a PBX/Key IR. The title usually went to the older guys who had been around awhile. PBX/Key men did not generally climb poles one of the perks that came with the job. The younger guys never resented this because they respected age and had hopes of getting there themselves one day. So, Harry had his extension ladder leaning up against the building when I arrived. I went up the pole and hung that end while he took care of the roof attachment on the building. When I got down from the pole, Harry asked me to go up on the roof to check the building attachment, just to make sure he had the proper slack in the drop. So, I climbed up his ladder and went over to the mast where the drop was attached. It looked good to me and I walked back across the roof towards the ladder, but there was no ladder! I looked for Harry, but there was no Harry. I looked for his truck, but there was no truck. That son of a gun had taken his ladder and left me up on the roof! Fortunately, I was young and resourceful and found a way down by swinging over the edge and hand-walking down a power riser. When I returned to the work center that day Harry, and about 10 of his buddies, were waiting to have a big laugh at my expense. I had the last laugh though (sort of) because Harry had left his needle-nose pliers on the roof that day. After keeping them for a couple of days, I returned them to him (after some amount of begging on his part)!

The missing pliers incident above brings up another point. Tools were considered very precious and it required a monumental ordeal to get a replacement. Guys would do almost anything to avoid having to go through the process. First, there was the required "Missing Tool Report" that had to be filled out in triplicate. Next, the form was taken to the foreman for his signature and an oral debriefing of what happened to the old one. Then came the lecture about what you should do to prevent it from happening again. Then the signed form was taken back to the tool room window (tools were kept under lock and key and managed by the storeroom personnel). Very often, the storeroom guy would give you his two cents worth about the high cost of tools and how many were being lost. As a result of all of this 3rd degree, guys would go to any length to avoid the whole process. If all the lengthy and embarrassing procedures were intended to keep tool loss to a minimum, it worked!

Speaking of embarrassing, Pete Carpenter was installing a new service for a lady customer. Earlier, Pete had greeted the lady at the door, questioned her about the location of the telephone and begun his work in the normal manner. Later, Pete had just come down from the pole in the back yard when the lady and her husband came out of the house and walked toward him. As they got nearer, the lady said to her husband, "See there! He has been going around like that ever since he's been here!" In making her remarks, all the while her eyes were directed at Pete's lower-mid section. Naturally surprised and flabbergasted by all of this, Pete looked down and noticed his pants zipper was down. After quickly zipping it back up, Pete apologized and explained he had not been aware it was down. The husband then said to his wife, "Is that what you called me home for? Good grief woman, the man didn't even know about it and it's no big deal anyway!" "Well it was to me and I wanted you to see it!" she said, now somewhat sheepishly. "Go on back to work, son. I'll stick around until you finish" the husband said. IT TAKES ALL KINDS, huh?

Hodgson Thompson certainly qualifies to make the "Character List". Hodgson was working at a funeral home installing an extension telephone in the room where the embalming was done. The room spelled of formaldehyde and there were stainless steel tables and all of the "tools of the trade" hanging from the wall. All of this caused old Hodgson's hair stand up, but he reluctantly continued his work. He had just gotten the phone mounted and connected when it began ringing. It caught Hodgson by surprise! The caller, thinking he had reached the funeral director asked, "My mother-in-law just died! Would you recommend embalming her, cremating her or just burying her?" Hodgson said, "Do all three, don't take no chances!"

Guy Hammond, Sam Templeton and I were installing a 1A2 Key System in a marina. The showroom of the business was built out over the water supported by pilings. We naturally saved the hard part until last, but time finally came when we had to go under the building to run some cabling. We borrowed a small boat from the marina, loaded up our cables and tools and paddled our way under the building. Guy was standing up, reaching high above his head, nailing some cable supports to the floor joists. Out of the blue, old Guy fell over backwards out of the boat and into the water. Now, it wasn't very deep so there was no danger of drowning, but when Guy hit the water, all heck broke loose! His big splash had startled a seven-foot alligator, which had been snoozing nearby. That "gator" came alive and slapped the water with his mighty tail that sounded like 12-guage shotgun going off. Guy was back in the boat in a nanosecond, white as the backing on a roll of rubber tape! Afterwards, he said, "I was having a 'Maalox' moment!"

Sam Brown had his moment as well. He was on a job away from his home base with a half dozen other Splicers. They were staying at the Skyline Motel which had been a fine motel in its day, but no longer. In fact, it had the reputation of attracting a fair number of "ladies of the evening". One day when classes were over and everyone had eaten dinner, we all came back to the motel. Sam retired to his room, got out of his clothing and was lying on the bed watching TV.

Sometime thereafter, there was a knock at the door. Sam got up, clad only in his shorts (and half-asleep by this time) cracked open the door and peeped around. A beautiful young lady was standing there and asked if he would like some company. Sam, being half-asleep, thought it was the maid and let her in. He sat down on the side of the bed and suddenly she was sitting right beside him. Sam was beginning to wake up! It's important to note that Sam and the others had been out of town and away from home for about five weeks. It should be no surprise that Sam was homesick and feeling un-loved. Now, when the "lady" sat down beside Sam, she also began her amorous advances. Ever so softly, the "lady" said, "Do you want to do some business, Honey?" Sam replied with a somewhat shaky almost pleading voice, "If I obliged, Sugar, I'd to be out of business back home!"

Then there was the time when my friend, George Truman, was accused of drinking on the job. Poor old George came into the work center at the end of the day smelling like a brewery. It was so obvious, but no one said a word. Drinking on the job was serious business! The first time it happened, the foremen noticed it, but looked the other way. After all, George was a good telephone man and a respected family man as well. The following week, it happened again and that heavy odor of stale beer was all over old George. This time, his foreman made a note of it. In addition, he talked with the Supervising Service Foreman about it. Neither knew quite how to approach George about, so they let it go once again. Well, it was just a matter of time when George came in the third time once again smelling like he had taken a bath in rotten beer. George's foreman couldn't ignore it any longer. Remember "Bumper meetings"? That's when your foreman took you over to the back of your truck, put one foot up on the bumper and explained the rules of the game in great detail. "How can you come in here in that condition? Don't you know you can get fired for drinking on the job? This is the third time you've come in smelling to high heaven!" the foreman said. George was flabbergasted! "What! I haven't been drinking! What are you talking about?" George fired back. "Don't you think it's obvious by the heavy beer odor all over you!" returned the foreman. "Good grief!" George said. "That's because I keep getting called back on trouble reports from that crazy guy who makes beer in his bathtub!

The whole house is polluted with all kinds of stuff to make beer and his bathtub is always full and it sloshes out in the floor and gets all over me. Is that what you thought of me…that I was drinking on the job?" "Uh ah", the foreman stammered. "The crazy guy won't let anyone else work on his phone! He always asks for me! That's all there is to the whole thing! I wouldn't drink a drop of that stuff anyway! It wouldn't make good rat poison!" The "bumper meeting" ended with the foreman red faced and apologizing and old George steamed to the gills.

The term steamed reminds me of another story. Back in the good old days of working in Florida, before it became overly populated and when telephone people got a lot of respect, I recall working with Roy Barnes, a good telephone IR. I was riding with him for a few days as indoctrination before taking over his area prior to his transfer. The first day at lunchtime, we stopped at a roadside grocery to buy lunch. Roy suggested just buying a Coke and a loaf of bread.....he would provide the rest. I had no idea what he was talking about, but it was his lead.

Soon, we were parked overlooking a beautiful bay of blue water. Roy grabbed the bread and a small salt shaker from his glove box. He said, "Come on...follow me", as he walked out into the water. Dutifully, I followed and was introduced to one of the most memorable lunch feasts of my life. We were standing in about two feet of crystal clear water and right in the middle of a commercial oyster bed. Big, beautiful oysters all around as far as one could see through the water. I had to watch Roy open up a couple before getting the technique. He'd use his pocket knife, find an opening and pry them apart. Then, he'd cut the oyster away from the shell, hold it up to his mouth and let it slide right down. Ummmm good! After a few in that manner, we'd load a couple of them on a piece of bread, sprinkle salt on it, fold it over and gulp that down as well. Oh brother! I can still taste them now! They weren't steamed, but oh so good just raw! Normally, they shot anyone caught in those commercial oyster beds, but the resident telephone man got special treatment....life was good!

In that same general area, we had a good-sized submarine cable on the bottom of a narrow canal that separated the mainland and the beach. It was well-marked with signage as was always the practice. It wasn't enough! And, when does a boat, dragging an anchor always snag the submarine cable.....late at night of course! Oh brother! The whole beach community was out, so two line crews along with four splicers were called out to start the repair job. It was a large cable that interfaced with buried cable in manholes on each side of the canal. The splicing job required a good many hours..... a long intro' for the next story. The night was dark and cold. The splicing crew on the West side consisted of two old veteran Splicers, Harold Orr and Ralph Woods, who were long past getting overly excited about a thousand telephones out of service. Neither were they in any particular hurry to complete the job. They were on call out, making double time. They also came prepared to keep warm with their stash of moonshine in their lunch boxes. After a few too many swigs from their mason jar, they heard voices up top. Climbing up out of the manhole with heads somewhat foggy, they looked across the canal to the other manhole. Two women were there talking to the other splicing crew and looking toward Harold and Ralph. Harold squinted his eyes and said with slightly slurred speech, "Oh my goodness! That looks like my wife and my girlfriend!" With that, old Ralph said in similarly slurred fashion, "You know, I was about to say the same thing!"

Dames! Let's talk about Frame Dames. And, if you're a telephone type, you know that is not a derogatory title. Forever, the job title was Frameman, but when women came on the scene, the title had to be changed. The men had often been called Frame Hops or Frame Jockeys....not very appropriate for a woman; so, the term Frame Dame was coined. If a craft job formerly held by men was ever well suited for a woman, it was the Frame job! Women were generally smaller, could move around with greater agility, could pull a jumper or trace a circuit as good as a man or better......and they looked a whole lot better on a ladder!

My favorite Frame Dame was Iris Farmer. She was a former Operator who had bid on the job and to her surprise, got it! She had little idea what the job was all about, but she was a quick learner and soon proved to be good at the job. But, her early days on the job were not easy! Most of the outside guys enjoyed working with her; in fact, it was a very nice change to hear a female voice answer the frame line. For some though, it was too much of a change to handle and, they refused to talk with her. When she answered, they would ask to speak with one of the men. Recall, prior to that time, there were no women in the craft jobs. Some men saw it as a move to displace them with women. After a while though, they got to know Iris and accepted her as someone who could hold her own on the job. Thankfully, Iris kept a good attitude about the matter from the start and never openly complained about the chauvinistic-related problems.

Thinking of Iris reminds me of a story she enjoyed telling. She regularly worked with a Frameman by the name of Raymond McClure.

Raymond was about 10 years older than Iris and was a very quiet, sincere sort of guy. He was also very religious. You never heard old Raymond say any kind of off-color word much less a curse word. Well, one day Iris moved her ladder over top of Raymond while he was working on a low horizontal block. He was concentrating so much on his work that he had not noticed her doing so. Suddenly, he stood up and hit his head on that ladder. Iris came down and asked what happened. Raymond said, "Ummmm, I hit my head on that ladder and it's killing me!" Meaning to comfort him, Iris asked "Did you cuss?" And Raymond, still hurting, said "Ummmm, no, but if you'll write it down, I'll sigh it!"

Richard Jones reported to a work center that had a tool supply area enclosed in a heavy gauge wire cage. There was a window or pass-through that opened up during working hours to hand tools and supplies to the IRs. One day, Richard walked up to the window and asked the storeroom guy for a new screwdriver. The storeroom guy ("Wash" Brown) was far too conscientious! And, that day, he evidently thought he owned everything in the whole storeroom. He asked Richard if he had a Lost Tool Report. Then he asked if it was signed. Then he asked if Richard had looked for the screwdriver in his truck seat. Then he asked if he had lost other tools recently. Richard, ordinarily a jovial guy, was getting more steamed with each question. Finally, he said, If, if, if! If a frog had pockets, he'd carry pistols to shoot snakes with!

"Sir! Your wife!"

CHAPTER 6 - WHAT'S IN A NAME?

Shakespeare said it first, but it's worth some discussion here as well. In an early chapter, I wrote of a new guy who was labeled "Oops". It was traditional to give a nick name to almost everyone who was hired. Usually within a few days after arriving on the scene, somebody would recognize a unique characteristic about the new hire and stick a label on him. There must have been a million of them. You remember….they were Shorty, Too Tall, Fats, High Pockets, Yogi, Huckleberry, Spike, Judge (in my case), Beechfork, Pinky, Red, Brownie, etc. It didn't seem to matter if the new guy agreed on his new nick name or not. Once he was labeled, it stuck!

The nick name thing was also true with the power company. They shared this somewhat warped desire to give everyone a name other than his given one. In fact, they carried the thing even farther than we did. They had names like Green Teeth, Clam-Shucker, Stink Pot, Flat Bottom, Porky, Ground Bait, Snorkel Nose, and such! These would have been a little too descriptive for use in the more sophisticated phone business, don't you think?

We had a lot of other things in common with the "power boys" though. Each job was very important to the public. We used similar outside plant. We worked on the same poles. We used some of the same equipment. Each was considered a public utility and regulated by the same public service commissions. Perhaps the major difference in our jobs was that we worked with 48 volts and they worked with 48000 volts. Their work was a good bit more serious in that respect. On the other hand, ours was just as critical when someone picked up a phone (especially a red one) to make an important call. It's an age old debate. It's one of those "My dad can whip your dad" kinds of things. But, when the debate is over, we're still cousins and still friends!

Names are important! They identify people.....and things! Alexander Graham Bell was an important name in the telephone business. After all, he invented the thing! He didn't call it a do-hickey or a what-cha-call-it. He named it a telephone! And, most of the nation's telephone companies used to include Bell as a part of their name. There was Bell of New York, New Jersey Bell, Ohio Bell, New England Bell, Illinois Bell, Southern Bell, Indiana Bell and on and on. Then along came Judge Green, the Modified Final Judgment (it even sounds bad, doesn't it), the Consent Decree and Divestiture. Suddenly the name Bell was taboo! Suddenly we became Ameritech, U.S. West, Pacific Telesis, Nynex, etc. A few companies tried to remain tied somewhat to the Bell name such as BellSouth, Southwestern Bell and Bell Atlantic. Eventually they all lost any semblance of the founder's name, such as Verizon, SBC, Quest, etc.

The original parent company, AT&T, floundered for several years and was finally bought by SBC. Then SBC changed its name to AT&T and bought BellSouth. Whew! If that doesn't make you as dizzy as a termite in a yoyo, nothing will! It does, however, lend credence to the AT&T moniker even though far removed from the original company.

CHAPTER 7 - A ROSE IS A ROSE

Throughout one's lifetime, there are special people who come along and remain in the memory for life. Rose Satzke was such a person. She was a dear gal who managed an apartment building consisting of about 30 apartments. She was in her forties, which I considered old at the time I first met her. Rose lived alone and appeared to have a nice life.

At one time, Rose had worked for C&P Telephone Co. in the Commercial Department. Although seldom discussed, the old Commercial Department got most of the really attractive girls as soon as they were hired. They were the "contact" side of the business and were the first to meet with customers as they applied for service. Rose met the test for attractiveness as well as intellect.

By the time we met, she had lost her husband several years before and became sole owner of an apartment building, which she also managed. The building was near downtown and provided residence for mostly working singles. I would guess it to be worth about a half million dollars back in the mid fifties….a lot of money especially in those days! With that kind of net worth accompanied by her good looks and natural charm, Rose would have made some lucky guy a great wife. It was not to be. She was happy with her life and, although apparently lonely, was not looking for a husband or even a date!

Her apartment was downstairs and near the entrance to the building. She knew everything that went on and everyone who went in and out of the building. If there was a service order to be worked or a repair to be made, you had to see Rose either for a key or to get to the main telephone cable terminal which was in a closet inside her apartment.

Rose had a great figure for her age and was a pretty strawberry blonde.....almost red. An early morning installation or repair visit would always find Rose in her pink negligee. After getting to know me, she would let me in to check the terminal without giving her scanty attire a second thought. She was glad to have the company and enjoyed conversation. Most of the time, she'd hand me a cup of coffee or a glass of iced tea as I arrived.

After many visits and much conversation, Rose and I became good friends. Her bedroom was just off the inside hallway near the terminal closet. She had a long framed mirror on one side of the room, which reflected directly into her dressing room and bath area. After clipping to a cable pair and waiting my turn with the test board (sometimes it would take 10 minutes or more), I could not help looking into that mirror. Rose either didn't know of the reflected view or she didn't care. Oh goodness! Those minutes there in Rose's closet were so memorable and downright steamy. I'm sure I must have stood there with mouth open many times, but then the test board would eventually answer. "Test board!" "Uh, uh, uh!" "Test board..uh hello! Uh, uh, this is Judge"! Uh, uh, look at…uh 879-6431 and, uh, let me lift this… uh… jumper."

After finishing my work, I'd call to Rose to let her know I was leaving. She'd say, "OK, Dear" from a distance and I would leave. I left that town early in my career, but I have wondered many times what may have happened to Rose. She would be in her nineties now, if living. I'll bet she is still a doll!

Life is so short, isn't it! And as we make our way along life's journey, we leave so many things and so many good people without proper good-byes.

The following came from a company VP affectionately known as "The Bull". Many readers will remember him as Clint Perkins.

Life is a challenge - meet it.
Life is a gift - accept it.
Life is an adventure - dare it.
Life is a sorrow - overcome it.
Life is a tragedy - face it.
Life is a duty - perform it.
Life is a mystery - unfold it.
Life is a song - sing it.
Life is an opportunity - take it.
Life is a journey - complete it.
Life is a promise - fulfill it.
Life is a beauty - praise it.
Life is a struggle - fight it.
Life is a goal - achieve it.
Life is a puzzle - solve it.

Greater
Atlanta
Telephone Directory
Area Code 404
November 23, 1975
Southern Bell

A classic directory cover from 1975

Can you name them?

CHAPTER 8 - WOMEN CUSTOMERS

Yes, we almost always worked for women customers. That was a time when most women stayed home and kept house! After the big war the men came home, took their jobs back and women went back to housekeeping. They were our customers and we had to learn to deal with them! It was a dirty job, but someone had to do it!

Almost every morning of the work week, we were invited into a home by a woman in a housecoat! To a telephone man, it was just routine procedure! On second thought, it never really became completely routine. There was always the anticipation of an exciting visit with a cute little housewife. Years ago, the day of a housewife began by getting up early, getting their husbands off to work and their children off to school. Then they had their breakfast, washed the dishes, swept the floors, washed clothes, and fed the dog.....all the while (often all morning) in their housecoats.

Women in housecoats are a real case study. For example, some women would answer the door in a housecoat large enough and heavy enough for use as a splicer's tent. Then she would let a telephone man into the foyer and ask him to wait there until she changed her clothes. Two minutes later, she would return in short shorts and a little halter-top. Men, beware! Those sweet little things think differently than we do! What a job!

Part of the OJT (on the job training) for a rookie telephone man was learning how to handle these situations. An unsuspecting young installer could get into real trouble if not very careful. Generally, it took about a full year on the job before understanding what to do or not do to stay out of trouble. With enough experience, those early morning calls on housewives could be fun and interesting without going so far as to get into trouble or even unduly embarrassing the housewife.

Knock! Knock! "Who's there?" "Telephone Man!" "Oh! The door is unlocked, come on in!" So you open the door and go in. There is the cute little housewife in shortie pajamas pretending to be too busy to answer the door. In reality, she probably didn't want the neighbors to see her opening the door in shortie pajamas and inviting the telephone man in. What a job!

Now inside, she walks you to the location where she wants the phone installed. In the old days, there was very little pre-wiring of homes and JK wire was stapled around baseboards, etc. to a point where a connecting block and telephone would be installed. The dutiful installer would pull back drapes, move furniture or whatever was necessary to point out to the customer exactly where the wire would be run. This required frequently bending down and pointing and looking, etc. It should be no secret to anyone, that the front of a shortie pajama top gaps open widely in certain positions. Most would hold their hand up to prevent exposing themselves.....some would not! The experienced installer would keep his distance in the latter case.

Why is it that a woman will wear a housecoat around in the morning without ever buttoning or tying it around her? "It may be a law, I don't know", to quote the comedian, James Gregory. The modest ones would always hold it together, but there were a few who would try their best to tempt an installer in one way or another.

Then there were the ones who insisted on climbing the pull-down attic stairs to point out where the wires came in. Sometimes this could be a serious challenge. How could anyone pay attention to what she was trying to point out while also trying to avoid looking up? Again, experience taught that it must be handled with care and dignity.

Basements could be a challenge as well. In older homes, drop wire was brought into the basement and the protector was mounted on a floor joist. When you're in the basement and the door above is open with light shining through, the silhouette of a housewife at the top of the stairs can reveal perhaps more than she intended. Once again, the IR must give the impression of concentration on the trouble and not on the scene at hand. And the view could vary greatly with the transparency of the clothing. The thinner the housecoat or negligee and the brighter the light, the more experience and tact required by the IR. What a job!

The wise telephone man would allow his customer to go just so far; then exit the scene before trouble came along. Experience provided an innate sense of timing to know when to go back to the truck for something and allow the housewife to regain her composure. An extreme case might call for a trip back to the work-center or perhaps a lunch break. Usually upon returning to the customer's house, she would be fully clothed, busy doing housework and obviously a little embarrassed about the whole thing. The incident was never acknowledged in any way during the remaining time there. The job would be completed and nothing more came of it. Later, the whole steamy thing could be discussed over coffee with some of the gang, but names and addresses were never discussed. They were treated like conversations overheard while working on the lines, i.e. it was fun to listen (and against the law as we all knew), but nothing was ever repeated. In my many years working as an installer-repairman, test deskman, etc. I don't ever recall hearing telephone conversation being repeated except for a few words or phrases, which were never identified with anyone.

Tommy Millirons recalled an incident when he visited a residence to install an extension telephone. He was directed by the housewife to install it by the bed in the bedroom upstairs. Tommy gathered his tools and supplies and headed up the steps. When he got to the bedroom door, he was surprised to see a young teenage girl lying on the bed asleep. She was very scantily clad to say the least! Tommy hurried back downstairs and said to the housewife, “You’ll have to go wake up your daughter”. She said, “Oh, that’s alright, she always sleeps late”. You go ahead and do your work, you won’t disturb her. Then Tommy said, “Well, you’d better go tell her that I’ll be working in her room. If she wakes up while I’m working, it will frighten her.” The lady thought for a moment and agreed it might be a good idea. She went upstairs and Tommy heard her speaking to her daughter. After she came back down, Tommy went back up only to discover the girl still lying in bed with no cover. Tommy went back downstairs and said to the lady, “You need to go cover her up!” “Oh, I’m sorry. She must have kicked her blanket off? OK, I’ll go back up and take care of it.” After she returned, Tommy headed back up one more time. This time, the girl was still in bed, but she had a sheet over her. “I didn’t know what else to do, but to go ahead and do my work”, Tommy said later. It may have been an innocent thing or it may have been a risqué tease by the girl. Tommy handled it right, did his job and got out of there without further incident! What a job!

I had the good fortune of working in a college town. In those days, the dormitories had a whole line of coin telephones on each floor for use by the students. That was before cell phones and in-room phones. Those coin phones got constant use and were therefore a constant source of repair calls. The students learned they could stick pins through the station wire to make free calls. Or, they would try to use slugs instead of coins and jam the coin chutes. Full coin boxes, fortunately, were another constant problem. By the way, coin telephone service was a giant “cash cow” and therefore a tremendous money maker for the companies. We did our best to keep them working properly.

When there was a trouble report in the girl’s dormitory, we always had to enter at the front desk where they would announce our presence over the in-house public address system. For example, they would call out, “Man on the 4th floor, Man on the 4th floor!” That announcement was supposed to alert anyone on the 4th floor that a man was present. They were far too nonchalant about it! By the time I would get up to the 4th floor, the announcement was old news and forgotten about. The coin phones were located in a common area, but across from several of the dorm rooms. This advantageous location was the subject of many lunchtime discussions by the IRs. Even on a first time visit, the uninitiated IR had plenty of forewarning about the female students running down the hallways of the dorm with little or even no clothing. I never knew just how the local test board decided who would be dispatched on those troubles. I was lucky enough to get my share I think! I would have done those for free! No! I would have paid for them! What a job!

My favorite place to work was a little town we affectionately called Cowtown (I won't reveal its real name). Cowtown was about 15 miles away from the work center, so the boss didn't come around very often. It was a pleasant 30-minute drive and there was a great little donut shop with good coffee on the way. Cowtown had a population of about 2000 people, a bedroom community as they're now called. Half of the town's people were elderly and retired and half were the younger group of the working class folks. The husbands of the younger set got up every day and drove into the city to their jobs. This, of course, left all the young housewives at home alone which made for a very interesting situation for the resident telephone man. There was no other place like it!

I was given the area of Cowtown because the previous installer, Roy Barnes, who had worked it for several years, had just relocated. My first few weeks there were uneventful, but that soon changed. As the only telephone man in Cowtown, I quickly became known as the new Mr. Telephone Company. It was not uncommon to go into the Rexall Drug Store for coffee and have someone come in to ask if I could go repair their phone. They were supposed to call repair service of course; but, they knew they could get a quicker repair by driving around town until they found my truck. There was one such occasion that particularly stands out in my mind. As I was sipping my coffee at Rexall, a pretty young lady (Garnet Sims as I later found out) sat down next to me and asked if I could fix her home telephone when I finished. I told her that I had other orders to work, but I thought I could work her in.

I followed her home and we went inside. To my surprise, there were four other young women sitting around as if they were waiting for us to arrive. Garnet grabbed me by the arm and proceeded to introduce me to the "girls club" as the new telephone man assigned to Cowtown. Old Roy had told me quite a bit about Cowtown before he left, but he didn't tell me about this part. After the last introduction, little of which I heard, I'll never forget my response. "Well, what can I do for you ladies?", and they let out some of those "Yee-Haw" yells like the young girls do at a rodeo. It surprised me! The next few weeks could not have been more exciting. This group of girls had been friends all through school and had lived in the town all their lives. They had married young, had kids and were tied down to a life they didn't particularly like. So, they formed their "Girl's Club" to try to put a little spice back into their lives. Fortunately for me, they let me be a part of it. Over the next year or so, I was treated to numerous encounters with the girl's club. What a job!

The very next day, I got a trouble report at the Teague residence. Judy Teague was the local dentist's wife. She lived in the best neighborhood and drove a beautiful little yellow Triumph TR-3. Judy was probably the oldest in the girls club, but she was the prettiest. She was not a petite girl, but rather large boned. She was probably around 135 or 140 pounds, but not at all fat. She had beautiful light blue eyes, long blonde hair and always well tanned. Being a beach community, all the "club" girls were well tanned.

I'm sure Judy married her husband, the dentist, for money and status. He was a real jerk and there was no love in their marriage. Anyway, Judy came to the door in a conservative shorts and blouse outfit. Well, I stepped inside and told her how good it was to meet her and all the rest of the girls at Garnet's house, just trying to make conversation. Before checking the phone, Judy invited me to see her house. She walked me around showing me the kitchen first, then the pool and patio area, the den, and then the bedrooms. When we came to the master bedroom, she led me in and invited me to sit down on her new bed she had just purchased. I held my side tools up and sat down, but only for a second.

As a reminder, by this time, I was an experienced telephone man...not necessarily in years, but in experience dealing with overly friendly housewives. After the bedroom situation, I exited the room and left Judy on the side of the bed. I was heading toward the nearest telephone to check out the trouble report. There was no trouble. The line had good dial tone, it could be broken with the switchhooks as well as the dial, it was clear...no noise or hum…the line was ok. So I called the test desk and began waiting my turn to close out the report and get a new one.

After about a minute, Judy came into the room. She had changed her clothes and was now wearing a bikini bathing suit. I asked, "Are you going swimming?" She said, "No, I'm just hot!" I was on one knee and on the telephone located on an end table by the couch. Judy reached down to get a cigarette and lighter. I quickly picked up the lighter to give her a light. She held my wrist as she lit the cigarette and then moved the lighter and my hand back toward the table while allowing my hand to rub her thigh on the way down. There was so much bare skin within a foot of me that I hardly noticed what she had just done. Then she asked me to sit down on the sofa and immediately sat down beside me. Oh brother, she was something! Needless to say, I told the Test Board I'd call back. I had no sooner gotten the words out of my mouth when Judy climbed over on top of me, straddled my knees with hers and planted a long, juicy kiss right on the old kisser. At that point, I said, "Excuse me, but I’ve got to get back to work!” As I'm sure you'll agree there are just some things you don't do on company time. What a job!

A few days later, I had just stopped in a hardware store on Main Street to buy a new screwdriver (we bought our own tools in those days with General Tel). I was walking back across the street to my truck when Garnet pulled up and invited me over to her house for a cold drink. I hardly knew her, but there I was a few minutes later sitting at her kitchen table having a cold drink with her. She was the leader of the “Girl’s Cub” and quickly became my favorite. Tall, slender and well tanned, she was quite a knockout! What a job!

When it came time for lunch, I always headed for the beach. I could pull my truck up facing the beach and surf...a ringside seat for girl watching. The Cowtown girls were almost always there and would come over to my truck for conversation. There were five of the well-tanned beauties there one memorable day including Garnet Sims. As I have said, she was my favorite; probably because she was nearer my own age and had the best figure I have ever seen. This day, Garnet was especially friendly as she came over and sat down on the front bumper of my truck. That much bare skin, so close, never failed to get my attention. What a great lunch break! Plans were made for the weekend which turned out to be one for the books! What a job!

The following Monday, I was in the local Rexall Drugs for my morning coffee and Garnet walked in. She sat down beside me and ordered coffee. "How was your weekend?" she asked. "It just couldn't have been better! How was yours?" I asked. I could tell from her demeanor that something was wrong. She said, "It wasn't so good, I'd like to talk to you about it." I said, "Sure, go ahead!" "No, not here!" she said. "Come over to the house for lunch and we'll talk." I said "OK" and she left sort of suddenly without finishing her coffee. I was still thinking about it when I called in for my next order and was given a "DNP" (disconnect for non-payment) on Garnet's phone. Oh brother, I thought, this is not going to be easy. It was about 10:00am and I didn't want to face Garnet with this bit of bad news since I would be going over at lunchtime anyway. So, I waited a few minutes and called in the disconnect order as being completed. By noontime, I had completed my next installation order and headed for Garnet's house.

Garnet invited me in and I sat down at her kitchen table. She began to tell her story. It seems her husband, who always worked out of town, had stopped sending her money. She had some serious financial troubles. To make matters worse, he had called her to ask for a divorce. She told me she was going to have to return to her hometown and move in with her mother for a while. I didn't know what to say to her. I showed her the DNP order and told her that it caused me to suspect there was some kind of trouble. I offered to leave her phone connected until she had to leave, but asked her not to make any long distance calls. In this little town, the installer-repairman could do those kinds of things (although not legal) because I ran the office jumpers and decided the cable pair and number assignments, etc. It was a very small, unattended office, which meant there were no switchmen or framemen there on a full time basis.

Well, Garnet thanked me and said she would probably be leaving in a day or two. I expressed my sadness to see her go and asked if I could do anything to help. She said no and so I left and finished out the day. It bothered me that she was leaving because I had grown to like her a great deal. Also, it bothered me because I would be losing my best contact with the rest of the "Girl's Club". The next day, I dropped in on Judy Teague, the dentist's wife, to get her take on Garnet's situation. Judy was well aware of Garnet's problems and, in fact, told me that there was more to the whole thing than Garnet had said. It seems Garnet and her husband had been separated for only a short time and that her husband had their son with him. The son was Garnet's real concern, not her own financial trouble. Anyway, Judy said that she and the other girls were planning a going away party and that I would be invited.

The next day, Judy ran me down and told me to be at Garnet's house at about 3pm for the party. It was a hot day and I was dirty and sweaty by lunchtime. So, I drove home just to shower and change clothes, which I rarely did in the middle of the day. After returning to Cowtown, I tried my best to stay clean and dry until the 3pm party.

When I arrived at Garnet's house, it seemed strange that there were no cars in the driveway. I must have gotten the time wrong, I thought. Garnet was waiting at the door with a glass of iced tea and her very pleasant smile. I said, "Where are the others? Did I get the time wrong?" She smiled a little more and said, "No, you didn't get the time wrong, but the party's over and they've gone." "What do you mean?" I asked. "Well sweetie" she said, "I just wanted to spend some time on my last day with you". Oh boy! I could have fallen head over heels for that girl. Thank goodness she had more sense about it than I did. After many years, I still think of her often and wonder what happened to her. She left Cowtown the next day and I never saw or heard from her again.

I worked in Cowtown for about another year, but things were never quite the same after Garnet left. It's surprising what a difference one person can make in some situations. Thank you Garnet wherever you are!

What a job!

BELL TELEPHONE NEWS
FEBRUARY
1924

CHAPTER 9 - THE LOCAL TESTBOARD

The local testboard (later called the testdesk) was the heart and soul of telephone repair. It was usually located near the central office and consisted of cord boards similar to operator cord boards.

They were used extensively in the old days for testing telephone lines, isolating trouble sources and dispatching repairmen on repair calls. Take note of the attire…vests and ties, no doubt.

A call to the testboard would be answered on a line commonly shared by other installer-repairmen, splicers or linemen. In other words, an incoming call went right in on the conversation between the test deskman and whomever else he was working with. There were almost always others on the line waiting their turn to talk with the test deskman and all could hear the ongoing conversation. Everyone just waited his turn; and, listening to the conversation seemed to help pass the time. Actually, it was possible to talk to anyone else on the line even while the test deskman was talking to his current "client". It was like a party line with everyone on the line listening in at the same time. If the testdesk was very busy, a fifteen or twenty minute wait was not uncommon. The ability to talk to others on the line made the long wait more tolerable and broke the monotony. The test deskman could determine who was up next by keeping track of the order in which he put up the “answer” cords. Maybe you had to be there to understand it, but it was the early-days version of carrying more than one call on a single line (somewhat comparable to multiplexing these days except in real-time analog). Occasionally, the test deskman would have to say, “OK, cut the chatter!”, and all the waiting parties would be quiet for a little while so he could continue with his business. After a bit, everyone would begin talking again until the next scolding.

The testdesk was like an operator's cord board, but equipped to do various testing of telephone lines. A test "position" (as each section of the board was called) had a flat desktop where the deskman could make notes. Along the back of each position, there were several rows of toggle switches called shunt keys or test keys. These keys were used to test for shorts, grounds, foreign battery, etc. They could also be used to apply high voltage and tones depending upon the need. The board pictured above is an early one, but very similar to a later versions. The large round volt/ohm meter on the front of each position was called a Galvanometer. Also on the front (or vertical riser portion of the position) were several rows of jacks which corresponded to the number of incoming lines and test circuits available. In those early days, a testboard was quite an impressive bit of technology.

I had the good fortune of working on one of these boards for about a year. It was probably the most coveted job of all the "craft" jobs because a test deskman was respected for his technical expertise; and, it was a soft job, i.e. inside and out of the weather.

When a call came in, it caused a buzzer to sound off. The test deskman reached for a cord, pulled it up and out of its storage hole at the back of the desktop, plugged it into the jack which was lit up on the vertical riser portion of the desk, and answered "Testboard!" Some installer-repairman, cable splicer or lineman would be on the line, very often on a pole or in a manhole. He might be possibly half frozen, not in the best mood, and always in a hurry. In those days, we didn't have bucket trucks, so we were either on a stepped pole (if lucky) or on hooks. So, the test deskman tested the line by asking that the drop be lifted, or a short or ground applied. Sometimes a tone would be applied to the line so the IR could find his pair and pick it out of all the rest in the cable. And after the trouble was cleared, the repair ticket was completed as “Cleared” and the IR was given another trouble to go on.

On a busy day, usually a rainy day, there would be a lot of cable troubles. Back before air pressure and jelly-filled cable, a little bit of moisture in a cable could wreak havoc and put several hundred lines out at one location. Those were the days I enjoyed most. There was never a dull moment and time passed very quickly. The nice, pretty, clear days were sometimes very dull and uneventful. On those quiet days, each test deskman would keep his answer-cord in hand ready to jump at the next call to come in. That's when the days got long!

One form of entertainment on a slow day was eavesdropping on conversations at the local brothel. Getting up that number, although fun at first, quickly got old no matter how "spicy" the conversations were. Odd, after hearing a number of such conversations, they all sound about the same. And, having such easy access to them seemed to take the fun out of it!

A typical "Step" Office (long gone now)

Hello.....Frame......Give me my Number 1 Shoe on Cable 5, Pair 247. Sound familiar? If you were ever a Frameman, Frame-person, "Frame Dame" or "Frame Hop"……it should! "Frame? I'm waiting for my Number 1 shoe! Get with it please!"

By the way, the term "getting up a number" in testboard terminology refers to when the test deskman dials a number for testing. He begins by pulling out a test cord and plugging it into a "test circuit" jack on his board. Upon dialing the number, the line associated with that number then comes "up" on the large galvanometer on the front of his position. In other words, the big needle of the instrument would be activated and move from zero to whatever voltage characteristics existed on the line. A good test deskman could then determine if there was a problem.

Here's another testboard story. Russell Sanford, a fellow test deskman, was eavesdropping on clandestine arrangements being made for an out-of-town client at a local brothel. The client was to show up at an appointed time and be given the royal treatment. Seizing the opportunity, Russell got up from his test position and supposedly went outside for a smoke. He never came back that day. Later, we found out he went over to the brothel, told them he was the out-of-town client reporting a little early and took advantage of their hospitality at no charge!

The most common job of the local testboard was to test lines when trouble was reported. There were several ways it could be done. The test deskman could simply dial up (or get up) the number. From the testdesk, he could then "look" at the line, which meant he could see the line characteristics on his volt-ohm meter. By flipping several toggle switches (shunt keys or test keys), he could tell if the line was shorted, grounded, etc. Or, the line could be tested with a "shoe" on the cable pair. This was a device that had to be manually inserted on the main frame by a frameman inside the central office. It provided a means by which the testdesk could isolate the office and the cable pair; i.e., the test deskman could determine if the trouble was in the office or out in the field. The testdesk was equipped with a direct line to the frame. We called it the "hoot & holler". It was actually a two-way voice line to an amplified speaker near the frame. It allowed the test deskman to call for a test-shoe on such and such a cable pair, for example “Cable 8, Pair 31”.

A typical incoming call to the testboard would be answered with an "answer cord" or a "line cord" or "#1 cord"....they were called by many names. To the test deskman, it was a cord usually on his left as he sat at his position. The call would activate a buzzer and a small light bulb over a jack (hole). The test deskman would grab an answer cord and plug it into the lighted jack. Upon inserting the plug into the jack, the test deskman would flip a toggle switch on the flat portion of his desktop and answer, "Testboard!" or "Testdesk!" The caller would state his name and nature of his problem, usually a request to test the line that had been reported in trouble. "Where are you?" the test deskman would ask. "I'm at the terminal!" the installer-repairman might answer, which usually meant he was on a pole. Sometimes he would be at a terminal inside a building or maybe at the back or side of a building. "Lift your drop off!" the test deskman would say. "OK, it's off!" Then the test deskman would flip his toggle switches and test the line. Lifting the drop off would remove everything from the line, i.e. the drop wire from the pole to the house, the station wire, the telephone set, etc. If after lifting the drop, the trouble still existed, then the test deskman would probably get a shoe on the cable pair to remove the office equipment. If the trouble still existed, then the installer-repairman would usually have to call “Assignment” and get a new cable pair.

For those readers who are not familiar with this whole procedure, imagine a fifteen hundred pair cable getting cut by a contractor's trenching machine. Fifteen hundred lines dead and as many as six thousand homes out of service (four parties to a line were common in those days). If it happened instantly, a large cable getting cut could even lock up the office. Lock up was a term used when all switches were seized or activated. When a cable pair is shorted, the office switch thinks it is a customer telephone off the hook requiring dial tone. When a cable is cut, all pairs in the cable might be shorted and thus that many switches seized to provide dial tone.

For example, if a fifteen hundred pair cable is cut, the office switch thinks there are fifteen hundred lines calling for dial tone. So the office switches try to provide dial tone for all fifteen hundred. Imagine fifteen hundred switches activating simultaneously. In some small offices, this would cause the whole office to lock up and no calls from any other telephone could be made. If the cable had been nicked and water was seeping in very gradually, the troubles occurred in a more subtle, gradual fashion. An alert test deskman could spot such a problem after getting several reports in the same cable.

Another aspect of installation-repair involved the customers. In order to make maximum usage of cable, customers were continually being switched from one cable pair to another. Sometimes, only one or two customers were switched to make room for a new telephone somewhere. Other times, it was a larger "cable throw" done on an engineering job order. Either way, it was always possible in switching cable pairs to result in disconnecting a customer by mistake. Standard procedure was to call the customer before starting the throw as well as after just to make sure everything had been put back properly. Use of a "ring-back" code number to verify the number on the line was commonplace. Thus, the customer played an important part of keeping things straight in those days. It should be noted that today's telephones use an entirely different technology not even remotely related to the technology and procedures just described. Today, customers would almost never give their phone number to anyone calling, even if they identified themselves as a telephone worker.

The test deskman had access to any type of information about a telephone. By using the telephone number to find the corresponding line card, it was possible to determine the customer name and address as well as the cable pair and terminal serving him. Today, this might be compared with ANI and ALI (automatic number and location identification) which is widely used to provide 911 Service.

My good friend, Sam Templeton, recalls a story about our old fishing buddy and test deskman, "Freck" Neville. Freck had a small farm where he kept a few head of cattle.

After working on a cable throw with cable splicer, Terry Roberts, they agreed to meet for lunch and a beer down at the “Thumbs-up Bar”. And, after perhaps a few too many, they decided to drive to Florida and go fishing. It was a 350 mile drive one way. Off to Florida they went, very “overly-subscribed” to drink! Upon arriving at the Florida fish camp that evening, Freck had sobered up a little and came to his senses. He went to a telephone, called his wife and told her he would be a little late getting home. They drove all night to get back home. Early that next morning, Freck dropped Terry off at his home and went on home himself. Both reported to work that day and neither was ever found out! Reaction of the wives was probably a whole other thing, but never talked about!

The test-desk I worked on was located very near the service order dispatch desk. The dispatcher was John Stenson, a "temporary" who was actually a cable splicer. He had been injured on his outside job and they had brought him in on the service order desk just to get eight hours of work out of him. He was a religious fanatic and preached or sang hymns all day long!

One evening, I called the local "Dial-A-Prayer" from my testdesk position and patched the prayer over to his answering machine. I did this repeatedly for at least eight messages. By the way, the service order dispatch desk was among the first to use an answering machine to “pass” completed orders. The next morning, John came in and began to replay his messages. They, of course, could be heard by everyone in the office. And, everyone stopped work and looked at John. "What do you have there John?" someone said. "Maybe the good Lord is trying to tell you something John!" another said. By the third prayer, old red-faced John was frantically trying to find the end to the things. "Somebody has a sick sense of humor!" he said loudly, so everyone could hear. "I'd like to know who did that!" he mumbled, by this time much more quietly. I wish I could say that it cured him of preaching and singing. It didn't!

The local Testboards are long gone now just as the telephone dial, "Hello Central", green trucks, etc., but the memories are still there and are just as sweet.

In stark contrast to service in by-gone days, when my home phone went dead recently, I called Repair Service (after 101 questions and punching the options). They promised to be out between 8:00 a.m. and 7:00 p.m. Really? At one time, we had a two hour commitment for business service and a four hour time for residence! I asked if they could give me a smaller time window, but the impatient service person of middle-eastern descent said, "Would you like us to call you before we come?" I replied that I didn't see how he would be able to do that, since our phones weren't working.

"I don't care where you get it. Get me a scare-crow!"

At one point before the call ended, he also requested that I report future outages by email. Does email work without a telephone line?

(It didn’t in those days) Grrrrrr……

CHAPTER 10 – CUTOVER

Cutover was often the training ground for new linemen and installers. A new man could learn quite a lot without jeopardizing telephone service. A typical day of cutover might include a service drop transfer from open wire to new cable, dismantling an open wire lead, removing old drops, etc. Open wire "leads" (as we used to call them) consisted of a pole line and one or several cross arms. A cross arm typically had ten pins equipped with glass insulators (the type you see as collector items these days). Since a telephone line (circuit) required two wires, a cross arm could accommodate five lines (10 wires, 2 wires per line). In the early days, there were as many as sixteen parties on one line. So, a cross arm could conceivably serve as many as 80 telephones (16 X 5). Typically though, (depending upon timeframe) there were ten parties on one line and one cross arm of open wire therefore could serve 50 customers. If "fill rate" would allow, they were often kept at eight parties per line.

During the Fifties and Sixties, most open wire leads were replaced with cable. To reduce the number of parties per line, cable was the next phase in telephone technology and a necessary step in achieving "Universal Service". Aerial cables came in sizes ranging from

six pairs to nine hundred pairs. Buried cables were often larger and underground cables (in conduit) even larger yet. A maze of cross arms and open wire could be dismantled and replaced by one cable. And, the cable was more reliable and easier to maintain. It got progressively easier as polyethylene and better air pressure came along. It got even better when jelly-filled cable was introduced. These days, almost all cable is buried and/or in underground conduit. Customers should appreciate their phone service even more in times of bad weather disasters. Most often, telephone service continues to work when power and CATV services are down…..thanks to a bunch of "just old telephone men (and women)"!

Isn't that a great old photo above? It shows eight cross arms, several lead cables in "rings" and a wooden cross-box with both doors flung open. This was probably taken around 1930 and is one of my favorites. Notice the guy sitting on the bench seat in front of the cross-box. He appears to be wearing a vest and bow tie. He would almost have to be the foreman of the five guys above. In later days, that bench seat offered a great vantage point for watching pretty girls driving by on the road below!

Cutover required moving the termination of the service drop (the wire from the pole to the house) from the open wire to the new cable terminal. Usually, a service upgrade from multi-party to four-party or less was provided with the new cable. Occasionally, the upgrade was not desired by a customer, (there were always a few customers who would not upgrade in hopes of being left on the party line by themselves while paying only the party line rate). We, of course, had ways of grouping those customers together on a cable pair that appeared at multiple terminals in tandem. Thus, we were usually able to keep the party lines full and at the level of service the customer was paying for.

The actual service upgrade from open wire to cable (a new line with fewer parties) required a cooperative operation between the central office and the cutover crew. Sometimes a change of telephone number was necessary. Before the drop was to be moved off the open wire to the cable, the cutover crew would call the "Frame" (the central office) and request that the new cable pair be turned up or "made hot" (the new line and/or number working on the new cable pair). Sometimes, the drop wire would be long enough for the move sometimes it wouldn't. If the drop would "swing" (long enough to move from the open wire to the new cable terminal) then the customer would be called and told the service would be "out" for a few minutes. Then the drop wire would be moved and tested and the customer would generally be called to verify that the line was working properly. If the drop would not swing, a "101B" box would be mounted on the pole where the old drop could be terminated. Then a "jumper" (usually a two conductor bridle wire) would be terminated at the 101B box and also connected to the terminal.

Cutover also refers to the conversion of one type of switching to another, for example from non-dial (operator handled calls) to dial. Recall the old wooden wall telephones? They were almost always associated with "magneto" (turn the crank on the side and wait for an operator to answer) type of service. When electromechanical switching came along, operator handled calls (except for long distance) became a thing of the past. Cutover of these areas to dial involved the changing of magneto and/or non-dial telephones to dial equipped instruments. I recall one office where the old wooden wall telephones were removed and piled high in back of the work center and burned! Oh what I wouldn't give for all of those old telephones now! What were they thinking?

After cutover and all customers had been moved to the new cable, the next step was to remove the old cross arms and open wire. A cross arm equipped with pins and insulators, weighs about a hundred pounds. The rookie telephone man, new to climbing poles and not yet feeling comfortable on "hooks" had his hands full when pulling the cross arm off the "thru-bolt" and lowering (or dropping) it to the ground. Visualize the lineman on hooks standing on a pole with safety strap around the pole. He is leaning back in his "belt" with his waist about eighteen inches from the pole. Many times, a new man would lift his first cross arm off the thru-bolt, be surprised by the heavy weight of the thing and immediately let it drop on his safety strap. That would surprisingly put all of the weight of the cross arm on the safety strap and also on his legs and hooks. He would literally be pinned to the pole and unable to move! If he was extremely strong (and most were) he could lift it off and free himself; otherwise, he would have to be "rescued". This, of course, was before bucket trucks became available.

Having to be "rescued" was something a rookie did not want. It was considered a negative reflection on manhood as well as intellect. One incident I recall involved a new man whom I had known throughout my childhood. Gary Houckman was a neighborhood bully and someone the other kids avoided. Of course, by the time he and I were hired by the "phone company", those feelings had passed and we were good friends. One day, he was working in a rural area about 15 miles out of town. He was installing a new service in a farmhouse, which sat several hundred feet from the road. A "drop" pole had been placed to support the extra long drop wire from the pole line along the road to the farmhouse. Drop poles were very often Class 9 poles, which were very small in diameter and had no other attachments. Climbing a Class 9 pole was a strange experience to say the least. First, it is very small and feels like climbing a toothpick. And, when there are no other attachments to constrain movement, it sways with the breeze when climbed. Once at the top, driving a "J" hook (1/2" X 5" steel lag bolt-like hook) with a lineman's hammer is like riding a bucking bull. If you don't coordinate hammer swings with pole sways, you will be thrown off! Gary managed to get up the pole and he got the "J" hook started. But, by that time, he was so shaken with fright; he could not get back down. He was so nervous he could not control his movements. Probably anyone who has ever climbed can relate somewhat to the feeling. Knees actually shake and feel like rubber. And, in Gary's defense, it should be said that it is much easier to climb up a pole than to climb down at least in the early learning stages of the rookie climber. So, Gary was stuck! Fortunately, he had made the drop wire "hot" before taking it up the pole, so he "tapped" into the drop wire with his test set and called his foreman. He was later rescued with a ladder and lived (although red-faced) to tell about it. His bullying days were long forgotten after that day!

Safety, quality and quantity were drilled into us on a daily basis. Safety meetings first thing in the morning came at least once a week.

Quantity was tracked by various methods (such as "work units") and was regularly displayed on a bulletin board in a prominent place in the work center. Quality was the more subjective measure and commonly done by the foremen doing "quality checks". All the craft people hated them, especially when they had to go back on a job to correct an irregularity. At times, the intimidation towards quality work got so bad that workmen were constantly looking over their shoulders. They felt like they were being watched as they worked; and, sometimes they were! The most dreaded part of the job was having a foreman pull up in his car to make a quality check while you were on the job. Most everyone hated to wear safety glasses too. In hot weather, they would fog up and get on your nerves worse than a "gaff" in the leg!

Once, while working cutover in a rural area, there were three of us on one pole. We were dismantling some open wire and cross arms. Someone noticed a "telephone green" car parked a half block away. In the most nonchalant manner, one turned to the others and said, "Don't look now, but that's Ed (a foreman) down there keeping an eye on us, just lurking and waiting until we make a mistake." Someone else said, "Let's let him know we see him. On the count of three, let's all pull one leg out (one hook from the pole) and hold it out in the air and salute at the same time." And so, on three, we all turned toward Ed, held out one leg in the air and gave him a military salute. After the car quickly started up and drove away, we all had a good laugh! Old Ed never acknowledged the incident.

BEFORE BUCKET TRUCKS

CHAPTER 11 - OPEN WIRE

Many of the fond memories of cutover also involve open wire, the original facility that first carried telegraph and later telephone service. The term open wire comes from the fact that the iron or copper conductors were bare wire, i.e. they had no insulation covering them. And, because of no insulation, they were always mounted on glass insulators to isolate them from the wooden pins and cross arms. Wood is a fairly good conductor of electric current particularly when it is wet.

The glass insulators have become collector items over the years and some (depending on color and type) are worth several bucks. If you are lucky enough to have one, just think what you may actually have. You could have something that carried an important call at one time. For example, I have a few that were taken from the old Jacksonville/Key West Toll Line in Florida. When Harry Truman was president, he spent a good deal of time in his winter home in Key West. My insulators probably carried his calls back to the White House. Maybe it even carried the call that OK'd the atomic bomb drop on Japan, who knows?

I loved working on open wire. It made me appreciate not only how things used to be, but also how much progress had been made. Open wire was like a link to the past and to the telephone men of another day who built the original system. The first thing I enjoyed doing after climbing up the pole and securing my safety belt was to strike one of the wires with a metal tool such as a big screwdriver. Then, I could watch the motion of the wave from pole to pole and listen for the echoes from the original sound. The wave could be followed by sight from my pole to the next pole and back again. And, it made a unique "twang, twang sound each time the wave went back and forth. It was like seeing "frequency and amplitude" with the naked eye (I know it's called Hertz these days). The longer the span, the longer the wave and the longer it took to get back to you.

The tools of the installer-repairman for working on open wire consisted of slack-blocks (a block and tackle with specific hardware grips for use on wire), a good set of lineman's pliers, a magneto test set (black wooden box equipped with crank-type magneto) and a sleeve roller.

Hardware consisted of iron or copper splicing sleeves, bridging sleeves, a coil of wire, spare glass insulators, tie wires, and sand paper. All of these things along with side tools, installer's test set, body belt and safety strap, lineman's wrench, lineman's hammer, ditty bag, set of hooks (climbers), and a couple of hand lines (ropes) weighed about a ton. Imagine climbing up a pole with all of these things attached to your body. That's why the job was a man's job and a strong, young man at that!

The above description of tools leads us to a discussion of a trouble report on a toll line. Trouble reports were commonly an “open” (usually a wire down), a short (one wire crossed with another), a ground (tree or guy wire touching a wire), or a swinging short (periodic shorting due to wind or tree branch). First stop was often the cable terminal pole that fed the wire. Lifting the open wire connector from the line terminal posts would prove the trouble either in the cable or the open wire. And, it was almost always in the open wire! Open wire routes normally took the shortest distance from one point to another. In other words, they did not always follow roads! So, after getting all the gear together, you had to start walking. From the road where you parked your truck, you might climb over a fence (after checking out the other side for a ill-tempered bull), you walk across a wide pasture, then up the side of a hill, back down into the gulley, across a creek, up the next hill....all the while carefully examining the toll line above. After a mile or so (if you're lucky) you come upon the downed wire. It's only one wire so it was probably shot by a hunter. A fallen tree would have taken out several more if not the whole lead. You take one end of your slack-blocks and attach it to the field-side wire. Then you attach the other end of the blocks to the office-side wire. You attach a hand-line to the slack-blocks and begin climbing up the pole. As bad luck would have it, downed wires were seldom from the bottom cross arm, but rather from one of the top ones, the hardest to get to! That's one of those "Murphy's Law" things! It also applies to the pin position. It seemed that the downed wire was always on pins one or two…or pins nine or ten, the farthest ones from the pole and hardest to reach! So, you climb up through lower cross arms being careful not to snag a wire with your side tools. You also hope to avoid coming in contact with a wire while there is ringing current coming through (have you ever tasted copper?). You get to your cross arm with the missing wire and safety off while also trying to maneuver to a good working position. You can now hoist up the slack-blocks being careful not to cross up the wires with existing wires. You then begin pulling the slack-blocks and bringing the two wire ends back together. When they are close enough to meet, you clean off the ends, dig out a wire sleeve and put it on the ends of the two wires. Next, place your sleeve-roller over the sleeve and begin turning the handle. Slowly, the sleeve-roller moves along the new sleeve while crimping it tightly around the wire ends. At this point, it is absolutely critical to position the sleeve roller squarely on the sleeve or else it will cut through the sleeve as well as the wire. The next critical test comes when you remove the slack-blocks. This is the supreme test of the holding strength of the newly rolled sleeve. If it did not get done properly, the wires will come loose and you will watch both ends go flying back toward the next pole and hit the ground. Then, it's the same wire raising procedure all over again......bummer! But, after experiencing that scenario one time, you never let it happen again! That's a rookie lesson you only have to learn once!

Once the wire is back up, spliced back together and properly tied at the insulator, then it's time to test it out. You swing your magneto test set around and connect it to the trouble pair. You also clip onto the pair with your Installer's Test Set and begin turning the crank (much like cranking an old wall telephone to get the operator). If all is well, an operator answers. You have no way of knowing which end to the toll line has answered, i.e. which operator in which town. So, you identify yourself and ask the operator which town she is in. If in your home town, then you ask her to connect you to the local test desk. If she is in the remote town, she will have to call an operator back in your home town who then calls the test desk. After reaching the test desk, you identify yourself and your trouble report and they can complete the test to verify the line tests OK. Then, it's back down the pole, again being careful not to snag a wire. After a long walk back to your truck, you head for the nearest general store for a Coke! That's a long explanation, but I wanted to provide some understanding of shooting trouble on a toll line. Actually, it often was a lot more complicated than the above and required a great deal more work to restore. Remembering those days makes me truly appreciate a warm home and lazy days of retirement!

This old photo also makes me appreciate retirement! Brrrrrr…….

Climbing expertise sometimes came slowly. It was easy for some and very difficult for others. Even after a new man became reasonably adept at climbing with full gear, he still had a considerable learning curve before he could work effectively on a pole. There is nothing any more artistic, even poetic, as the movement of a good lineman who knows what he is doing on a pole.

Recall the job of the rookie groundman (grunt) who remained on the ground to toss up needed tools or material. With a little practice, a good groundman could lay anything right up to the fingertips of the man on the pole. But, until they gained that much needed ability, thing could get almost dangerous. This reminds me of a time when Chuck Henderson was hanging a cross-arm. He was safety'd off and already had his cross-arm mounted on the thru-bolt. Somewhere in the process, he had broken one of the insulators, so he told the groundman to go to the truck and get another one. The groundman promptly did his duty and came back with a new insulator (about a full pound of solid glass). Chuck had a hand line dangling from his belt to the ground, but he did not have a bag attached to it. Rather than send him back to the truck, Chuck just told him to toss it up to him. The groundman took it in hand, carefully took aim and tossed it underhanded right up into Chuck's crotch. 'AAaahhhh! Ummmm...what in the world are you trying to do.....kill me? As soon as I get off this pole, I'm going to skin you alive! You better not be around when I come down! Ohhhhhhhhh! Ummmm!" After daily apologies for the next year, that groundman eventually became Chuck's best buddy!

As mentioned before, the original toll lines (open wire lines that carried long distance calls) sometimes took the route of a straight line from one town to the next. In other locations, they followed a road or a railroad. In any case, the route was often impossible to reach by truck. On those routes, the repairman had no choice but to park his truck (at the point where the toll line left the road) and begin walking the line. After loading up with the aforementioned tools and hardware, he weighed about a hundred pounds heavier for his trek across pastures, corn fields, creeks, and even mountains. If the toll line crossed a road again, say five miles from where he started, then he had to guess where best to park his truck for the shortest walk to the trouble location. It was almost impossible to make the right guess. If the trouble was located a mile from the far end and he started from the near end, then he had a four mile walk in each direction. In the latter days of open wire toll lines, two men and two trucks were dispatched so a truck could be parked on both ends of the route. In addition, it became a much safer matter of business with two men on the job.

At times, copper wire became so valuable that it was very profitable to steal it, i.e. for those who were not caught, of course. After a toll line had been cutover, it was commonly left in place until another crew could dismantle it. And when all circuits were dead, it became a prime target for the copper bandits. Alarms were installed to alert the switch room when it was being tampered with, but this was rarely an effective deterrent.

Most troubles in rugged areas, i.e. narrow right of ways with trees overgrown, were caused by fallen trees and tree limbs. Commonly, this problem was associated with a violent rain storm, heavy snow or winds. I recall once after a heavy snow, I came upon a pole very remotely located down in a valley that had been pulled completely out of the ground and was suspended in mid-air by the wire. As the wet snow had fallen, it very gradually added so much weight on the wires that the pole was very gently raised out of the ground.

And one more mention of slack blocks is in order. Imagine rolling the sleeve on the farthest wire from the pole, i.e. number one or number ten pin (pins were numbered one to ten as viewed with your back to the central office). It required leaning over backwards in your body belt and holding the roller in place (way out on the end of the cross arm) while turning the crank. A few of the shorter men had to actually safety off on the cross arm in order to reach pins 1 or 10. That would require lying in the body belt while hanging from the arm. It hurts even to describe it! Maybe if we old guys had had a bucket truck back then, we wouldn't have so many back problems now!

Then there were the kids and or hunters who enjoyed taking pot-shots at the glass insulators. Being made of glass, they would shatter when hit by a shotgun load or a rifle shot. Many times, the wire was also hit and would, of course, fall to the ground. Even when the wire didn't get hit, the loss of the insulator would cause grounding problems, especially in wet weather.

Iron wire was prone to rust and copper wire was prone to corrosion. Actually, after considerable build-up, the rust and corrosion would act as an insulator. I recall going on a trouble many miles out from town. There were several farm houses being served by one bracket pair (two open wires on wooden brackets nailed directly to the poles instead of on cross arms – see photo to follow). The source of the trouble was due to a lightning strike, which had melted the wire. It had stretched and was hanging down so low it touched the ground. One section (one span between poles) was actually lying in a small creek bed. In spite of this, the line would still carry a faint conversation. Rugged stuff that open wire!

Fire was another big problem for open wire. Many open wire routes were along roads. A lighted cigarette thrown from a car could ignite the roadside brush and destroy several spans of open wire in a flash. Copper wire when heated by fire will melt like butter and look like spaghetti drooping down from pole to pole. Nothing left to do, but replace it entirely!

My good friend Gene Thornton tells of an experience while working on a rural open wire toll line. As mentioned earlier, toll lines did not always follow roads, but rather took the shortest distance between two points. Gene and his crew came across an old, very remote farmhouse that appeared to be abandoned. While working in the area, they noticed that periodically, a car would pull up to the old house and the driver would go around to the back door. In a few minutes, the driver would carry a box to the car and drive off. It didn't take a brain surgeon to determine that they were bootleggers running a moon-shine still. Gene thought about reporting it to authorities, but he had a job to complete first. Besides, it didn't say anything in the "practices" about reporting a still if encountered while on cutover. The cutover job got done and the still was never mentioned again. Later, Gene said he could imagine the headlines in the newspaper: "Telephone line crew summoned to court after reporting local moon-shiners to police. Judge orders federal protection for witnesses during trial".

In rural areas, there was a service known as a "K Line". There were other names for the same service, but basically it was a single line, generally on a bracket pair, which served several very small communities over a wide rural area. It was a multi-party line with one telephone located in each community. The telephone was commonly placed in the most centrally located general store. The owner of the general store was required to make a commitment to the community.

When a call came in for anyone within a predetermined area around the store, the storeowner (or designate) had to find that person and advise them of the telephone call. The call recipient would usually follow the storeowner back to the store, "ring" the operator and ask that the call be set up for completion. Seventy five years later, it now seems impossible that our country was once that backward with telephone service. But, it worked pretty well at the time!

< "K Lines" were still in service throughout the 1950s and probably into the 60s. This one is on a bracket pair and the pole looks like about a Class 9. It was much like trying to climb a toothpick! Note the "wire ties" hanging from his belt.

It is hard to believe that telephone service was once so little understood. Today's reader who is not familiar with the history of the business may have no idea how really backward our rural customers were about telephone service. It was commonplace to have to instruct them in the use of the telephone set after the initial installation. It may have gone something like the following: "First, pick up the handset then dial the desired number. No! You must lift the handset off the little black plungers first! No, you talk into the end that has the cord coming out. The other end goes up to your ear! No, wait! You have to spin the finger-wheel all the way around to the finger stop. Otherwise, you will get a wrong number. Well, that sound is called dial tone. It's supposed to be there! In fact, you should always listen first to make sure it is there before dialing. If you pick up the handset and hear someone talking, don't dial, don't listen, just put it back down softly and wait until the talkers are finished.

No, don't pick up the handset to wait for someone to call you. The phone won't ring unless the handset in resting on the cradle. Huh? The cradle is on the top, where the little black plungers are located! Oh, I'm sorry! I didn't mean to sound like I was losing my patience!"

CHAPTER 12 – LONG & SHORT RINGS

Who remembers having to listen to the number and duration of rings to determine if the incoming call was for you or your neighbor? On a ten-party line, five subscribers (customers) were on the "tip" side of the line and five were on the "ring" side (assuming the line was full). Each customer got his own ring plus four more (the other four parties on the same side of the line). So, a typical ring might be two shorts or two longs or some combination of longs and shorts. Sometimes, two or more households of the same family would be on the same party line. If daughter was next door visiting mother, for example, she could answer her own calls from Mom's house by listening for the rings. If a nosey neighbor wondered who was calling next door, she could wait until the ringing stopped and then pick up to eavesdrop. Later, some phones were equipped with a monitor type of switch hook (plunger). It was designed to allow a customer to lift the handset and check the status of the line without interfering with someone else dialing out. And, it worked well while at the same time encouraged eavesdropping. The receiver could be lifted and the conversation could be heard without being heard. In other words, the transmitter was not activated until the plunger was pulled up an extra notch from its normal position. A problem would develop, however, when several people would listen at the same time which caused the volume to go way down. Someone would then have to say something like, "I wish these nosey people would get off the line so we could talk!" Usually it

worked, because everyone on a party line was in the same boat, so to speak!

A 300 Type Western Electric Telephone Set
(One of the "workhorses" of its day)

….and the 500 Set, the next "workhorse" after the one above.

W.C. Smith, as a young boy, was home alone one day and decided to listen in on the party line. He had been told never to do that, but kids will be kids and W.C. figured it would be fun to do. The conversation was between two neighbor ladies who were having some difficulty communicating. It seems one was explaining to the other something about her "goat" and the other mistakenly thought she said "shoat" (a small pig). W.C. got so involved in the eavesdropping and frustrated over the misunderstanding, he felt compelled to jump in.....and so he did! "Can't you hear anything? She's talking about her goat, not her shoat!" he shouted. Needless to say, the callers recognized his voice and told his parents. Of course, he was scolded and told never to talk on that telephone again. Many years later, when he went to work for the telephone company, W.C. said he was still very shy about talking over the telephone.

Remember the old dials and finger wheels? You'd stick a finger in a hole and spin the finger-wheel around to the "finger stop". Rrrrrrippppp! Then you'd release it and it would return with a tick, tick, tick, tick, tick the number of ticks depending upon the number dialed. The return speed of the finger-wheel was dependent upon an internal governor, which required an occasional adjustment by a repairman. A call to the testdesk would be made from the telephone set in question. The test deskman would have the repairman spin the dial while he watched the make/break rate of the dial on his meter. Then according to the test, the dial would be adjusted for either faster or slower speed. This was a rather delicate operation using a small brass retainer that kept the governor in place while the speed was set (with a "dial" screwdriver, by the way). Dial speed was critical for correct dialing due to the central office switches being fairly sensitive to it. A fast or slow dial would reach wrong numbers directly proportional to the severity of the "off-speed" condition.

Cycle ringing was an alternative to the inconvenience of getting other rings on a multiparty line. I was introduced to it when employed by General Telephone. The "Bell System" ringers were one cycle (30 cycle I believe) and rang either on the "tip" side of the line or the "ring" side. Until going to work for General, I didn't know there was any other way. General used ringers of five different cycles: 20, 30, 42, 54, and 66. The ringing equipment in the central office was capable of generating ringing current using these different cycles. For example, Party 1 would have a 30 cycle ringer on the "ring" side and Party 6 would have a 30 cycle on the "tip" side. Party 2 and 7 would have a 42 cycle ringer on each side of the line, and so on through all parties. Thus, no one heard any ring other than his own. It was slick and worked well!

There was one down side, however, to the cycle ringing. Ringing voltages varied considerably. The Bell System generally used a ringing current of about 90 volts AC. Cycle ringing voltages, however, ranged from about 60 volts on up to about 166 volts AC, which would hurt when touched!

On a new service installation, the first thing the installer does is "find his line". Back in those days the installer would clip on to a working line with his test set, dial up the number being installed and use a metal "216-B" tool to "run the terminal" (short across the available lines) until he hit his line and broke the audible ring. This method would never do these days due to widespread "special services" that may be interrupted. Besides, test sets have improved to the point of having other methods available.

On open wire, finding your line was a little different. First, the two sides of the line were on glass insulators and about 10 inches apart. It was easy to clip on a line with the separate test set clips, but about the only tool long enough to short across the wires was a lineman's wrench, not always carried by installers. So, the "grab" method, adopted by most installers, was to simply reach across the lines until the ringing current was felt. Ninety volts AC will give a pretty good jolt, but not too much for young, tough guys. It's a different situation altogether with 166 volts, as was the case with cycle ringing. The first time I tried the "grab" method on 166 volts, I was severely jolted and held by the current until, thankfully, the ringing cycle ended. I "tasted copper" for several hours! It was a good thing old Alexander (or someone) decided on intermittent ringing cycles instead on continuous ones.

Many times, you've heard the phrase, "There's nothing really new!" The term "reselling" was coined after the courts decided that MCI (and any other company for that matter) could buy services from Ma Bell and "resell" them to MCI customers. Basically, it worked this way. MCI could buy "bulk" service (say a million hours of long distance service) at a reduced rate. Then they resold those hours (say 100 hours to each customer) at a higher rate. But, the higher rate was still lower than Ma Bell could sell them to their own customers. Why? Ma Bell rates were designed to recover costs not only of the large metropolitan customers, but also of rural customers. MCI did not have to serve the rural customers! That's a very short explanation of "reselling" just to get back to my original thought in the first place.

Reselling had been around for many years before MCI came in. It was rare, but reselling happened when a rural landowner had renters (or farm hands) living on his property who wanted telephone service. Because it was private property, the Phone Company would not build facilities without being compensated for the poles, wire, labor, etc. As an alternative, the landowner would build his own facility. They were sometimes called "farmers lines" and in some cases consisted of wire on insulators on a fence line. The phone company would connect to the landowner's facility and provide service. The landowner was responsible for the service, but he would "resell" the service and charge a fee to his renters. The phone company was responsible for maintaining the line only to the point of "interconnect" (the first thing like modern day interfaces); but more often than not, the IR would get involved with a trouble even when it was on the farmer's private property.

Full coin boxes and the 3 C's were a constant test of moral values and company rules. Pay Stations (coin telephones) got a great deal of usage (before cell phones) and were a great source of revenue for the companies. They were "collected" regularly, but sometimes a repair call was necessary due to a full coin box. Inside a coin telephone, there is a coin chute, a collection relay and a coin box (in the most basic terms). A deposited coin drops down the coin chute, trips a switch that signals the central office to

provide dial tone. Then the coin drops on top of the collection relay until the call is completed (or not completed). At that time, the relay either dumps the coin into the coin box (completed call) or back down to the "coin return" (incomplete call). When the box gets full, coins start backing up and eventually will render the phone useless. All IRs carried a key to unlock the upper housing and provide access to the coin chute, relay, etc. The coin box was locked in place and could be accessed only by a "Coin Collector"(separate job title). Only in rare cases did the IR collect a full box; and it would be delivered immediately to the Business Office. Generally, though, he simply had to gather the coins from the chute and relay and install an "Out of Order" sign on top until the Coin Collector could get there to unlock and collect the box. Upon removing all of the coins from the upper housing, the IR would put them in a specially marked envelope and take it in to the work center at the end of the day.

The Three C's question arose when coins became lodged in the coin chute. If they were jammed above the dial tone switch when the customer deposited his money, then they did not provide dial tone. In other words, the customer simply had lost his money and never made a call. Who then should claim that money? The company always maintained that it belonged to them because the customer would be reimbursed if the request were made. Also, the money was essentially on company property. Good arguments! Nevertheless, there were questions enough in the minds of some to justify their pocketing the money. And, as usual, the company was ever mindful of this situation. Since the Three C's was such a serious matter, the company would occasionally "plant" a full coin box and report the trouble in the normal fashion. Then, they would wait to see who among the IRs was honest (or dishonest, as was sometimes the case). Alas, some unknowing IR would be sent home with days off without pay. In extreme cases the poor guy was fired, thus ending his phone company career with a severe blow to his integrity.

CHAPTER 13 - OPERATORS

< Oh yes! They were as pretty then as the young girls are now!

Emily Sue passed away and Bubba dialed the Operator. The Operator told Bubba that she would send an ambulance out right away to pick her up. "Where do you live?" asked the Operator. Bubba replied, "At the end of Eucalyptus Drive." The operator asked, "Can you spell that for me? "There was a long pause and finally Bubba said, "How 'bout if I drag her over to Oak Street and they can pick her up there?"

1880
IN 1880 TELEPHONE OPERATORS' HEADSETS WEIGHED 6 POUNDS! TODAY THEY WEIGH ONLY 17 OUNCES!

This was found in a 1940 Bell Company Publication. Today, they weigh an ounce or less!

A Man came home and found his house on fire, rushed next door, dialed the Operator and shouted, "Call the Fire Department. My house is on fire!" "OK," replied the Operator, "how do they get there?" And the man said, "Gosh, don't they still have those big red trucks?"

A lady saw an elephant out in her cabbage patch. She had never seen an elephant before so she dialed the Operator and said, “There’s some big thing out in my cabbage patch picking up cabbages with its big long tail”. The Operator said, “Well, what’s it doing with them?” The lady said, “ If I told you, you’d never believe me!”

There must be millions of stories about the experiences of Operators. They were a unique bunch! Each had their own way of answering calls: Opp'-rahter! Or Oper-A'-tore! Or Op'-er-ater! Some had a sweet, helpful voice. Others had an "I'm very busy, what do you want" type of voice. After a brief taste of some operator training, I quickly gained a great deal of respect for the work they did. I found that my experience on the local testdesk was little help in trying to do the operator's job. Fortunately, I never had to do it!

The older operator boards were equipped with answer cords (much as the local testdesk, but with far more cords). Having “all cords up” referred to a very busy condition when calls were so heavy that the operator had no more cords with which to answer calls. This did not mean she could take a break, far from it. She had to watch for disconnects and/or customers flashing for one reason or another. She always had piles of paperwork to do or catch up on.

She had to be acutely aware of the calculagraph (clock/call timing device in photo) in front of her. She always felt like the Group Chief was standing behind her waiting for her to mess up. She always wondered if her position was being monitored and if she would say the wrong thing at the wrong time. She was never free to leave her position until an appointed time, regardless of nature's call or other problems.

A caller to an information operator said, “I’d like the number of the Thens Bar and Grill.” The operator said, “One moment please”......paused and said, “I’m sorry, there’s no such listing. Are you sure of the spelling?” The caller said, “Well, it used to be called the Athens Bar and Grill, but the A fell off their sign!”

Then there was the caller who was trying to locate a sweater manufacturer in Woven. The operator said, “Woven? Are you sure?” And the caller said, “That’s what it says on the label....Woven in Scotland!”

What about the old guy who called in everyday to ask the same question. He had a German accent and his question was, “Ha-low Ah-par-ay-tore! Do you half a goot number for me today?” The operators never knew quite how to respond until one day when Opal Kitchens thought of the solution. She very politely gave him the number of a local brothel. He was never heard from again!

The operators job had its ups and downs, i.e. it could be anywhere from completely boring to very exciting. It could also be hazardous! Another operator story happened in a college town. It was a typical day, everyone going about their business. It was at a time when building security was hardly a thing to be concerned about. The doors of the company buildings were not always kept locked especially those most often used by employees. Often there were several different departments working in the same building, going in and out all day long. Well, on the eventful day of the story, an irate husband walked into the building and into the traffic room, walked up to his wife as she sat at her position, pulled out a pistol and shot her stone cold dead! True story! Who said being an operator was a safe job?

For a short time, I had the good fortune of working in an area served by a "Manual" office. The term refers to manual switching, i.e. operators on cord boards. Most manual offices were on their way out during the 1950s, generally replaced by new cross-bar or step offices. The operators of that day were special people to say the least. Many had been with the Company for a long period and had a great deal of experience with the telephones in their community. In the little town I was assigned, the operators did the repair service as well as dispatch.

Just imagine the scenario. There is no work center, just a small building used as a storeroom for telephone hardware. There is one telephone hanging on a wall. You're told to call the operator for the day's trouble reports. "Operator" the voice on the other end says. "Uh, this is Judge. I'm the Installer/Repairman on loan from Big-town. Do you have any troubles?" "Oh, hi Judge...welcome to town! Just a minute! Let me check! Yes, I've got one out on Brown's Branch Road. Do you know where that is?" "Yes, I think so", I'd say." "It's an NDT (no dial tone) and it sounds like a dead short!" she continues. "The name is Hershel Brown. He's the third farmhouse on the left after you pass the feed store. The number is 617W and he's on pins 7 and 8. Now listen, after you get on Brown's Branch Road, start counting the spans. Go to the fourteenth span with the big oak tree out in the middle. That's where you'll probably find the wires wrapped up in the tree." Don't chuckle too loudly! Most of the time, she'd be right!

Operators were a part of the old Traffic Department. How fortuitous! In the old days, departmental names seemed to fit so well with the role they played in the business. Traffic referred to the "traffic" of telephone calls placed and received. Engineering was engineering! Commercial was the business office! Marketing was the sales department! Accounting was accounting and Rates was rates! The Plant department was all things to do with plant facilities (inside or outside). And, following those lines, titles were just as simple and understandable, i.e. Marketing Manager, Commercial Manager, Plant Manager, etc. Nowadays, difficulty in determining the departmental role from the name is surpassed only by the near impossibility of determining what an employee does by his title. Somewhere in the Bible, God got very angry with the people and confused their languages resulting in all the different languages throughout the world. Likewise, when Uncle Sam (and his Judges, lawyers and politicians) got angry and decided to break up Ma Bell, they must also have confused the Company CEO's. After divestiture, apparently it wasn't enough to ask the employees to work longer and harder in dealing with the new company environment. No, they also had to gum up the works with meaningless departmental names and job titles!

Here's another great old photo. It was serious business! The Group Chief (sitting at desk) made sure of that!

Despite the strict working environment, operators loved their job. They understood that rules were necessary. They also understood the Group Chief's job and responsibility.

We are the unseen - ever watchful, never sleeping,
Binding the atoms together.
Not ours the glory or applause
We wear no uniform - and yet
Are a part of our land's destiny,
Guarding her secrets well.
We are the unseen - loyal - true to an ideal
One God, one country, one flag.
We want no praise, knowing out there,
Men have shed their blood that we might live
with others soon to follow them.
Our reward shall be - one day with the touch of magic
at our finger tips, to send across the quivering wires
One far-flung cry - "Ours is the Victory!"

Elizabeth Dayton Surry
Long Distance Operator
Washington, DC Timeframe - WWII

Sometimes we old telephone people tend to forget the many PBX Operators who worked for other businesses. They were just as much a part of the telephone business and telephone history as the rest of us.

I met one recently at a flea market. She said it was the best job she ever had. She also had the highest praise for Ma Bell and the many PBX repairmen she knew while working her board. The business world could not have made it without them!

CHAPTER 14 - DOGS, CATS, ETC.

Mike Snyder, the Country Music star banjo picker and comedian, once told the following story. Mike called home and asked his wife, Sweetie, if everything was all right. She said, "No! There are about 40 dogs out in the back yard." "Are they mad?" Mike asked. "Well, two of them aren't!" she said.

A three-legged dog walks into a saloon in the Old West. He sidles up to the bar and announces: "I'm looking for the man who shot my Paw."

Any old telephone man has had some encounters with animals from time to time. For one thing, there used to be a lot more dogs on the streets. There were a few leash laws, but they were rarely enforced; so, dogs running wild were common. Actually, the ones running wild were not the problem. Because of their freedom, they were generally pretty well behaved. The ones kept in fenced areas were the problem, at least to the telephone man. Fenced in dogs feel they have to bark a lot and protect their little fenced area of containment. And where are pole lines generally located? Well, right along property lines (and fence lines where the dogs are) of course.

Very often, fence builders use a utility pole to support their fence wire. It's not legal, so to speak, and we had the right to remove any and all "foreign" attachments from our poles, but we rarely did. Who wants to get a property owner (and customer) upset about such a thing? So, you put on your climbing gear and head for the pole. You see the fence and you see (and hear) the barking dog. You know you have to get up that pole one way or another. If you are lucky, you can hit it running and get up the pole and out of the dog's reach before he can bite. Sometimes, he's able to nip your boot before you can reach the second step.

The dog has been barking the whole time you have been working on the pole. You unconsciously stretch your work time trying to avoid the inevitable trip back down the pole where the dog is waiting. But now, you've got to face it! You've got to come back down! You think to yourself, this must be how a squirrel feels! With "hooks" on, it's easier to injure yourself coming down a pole than going up. You don't want to have to scurry down, but if you don't, the dog will bite you! You're thinking, if the stupid owner had any sense, she would come out back and call her dumb dog. You look toward the house, but there is no sign of the owner. You carefully reach around your back and pull your lineman's hammer from the belt loop. The dog is at the base of the pole, still barking, licking his chops and anxiously waiting for you to come down. A lineman's hammer has a hole through the head for use in turning pole-steps into the pole. You take aim through that hole at the dog's head, looking down the line of sight from above the hammer and down to the dog's head. Bombs Away! The hammer hits its mark and the dog is knocked out cold on the ground. "Oh brother! Did I kill it? What if the owner comes out now?" You scurry down the pole, get your gear off, and climb into the truck. Then you get back out of the truck, walk over to the pole, reach through the fence and pick up your hammer and "split the scene". You wonder about the dog's condition, but you're feeling pretty good about getting down the pole without getting bitten. Just the same, you don't want to be seen around there, at least for a while.

As luck would have it, a few days later, you get an order in the same area with the same pole and terminal assignment. You do a double take on the pole and terminal number; knowing full well you'll have to go up that same pole. After arriving at the location, you very quietly get your climbing gear on. You listen for the dog, this time secretly hoping to hear him bark, but hearing no sounds. "Maybe I killed it after all!" you say to yourself. You head for the pole, dig into the first step with your climber and BARK, BARK, BARK, BARK! That stupid dog is at it again, but this time, you're relieved. Thank goodness, he's not dead after all! So, now you've completed your work on the pole, you look down at the barking dog, you reach for your lineman's hammer and……

Because of the necessity of working on poles and/or terminals, a telephone man is required to be in alleys, back yards, pastures, fenced areas, etc. And, because dogs commonly reside in these areas, a telephone man had better gain an understanding of "dog nature". Each breed of dog has its own disposition and it helps to get to know them as soon as possible. There are some breeds you just don't mess with, such as Doberman, Pit Bull, Chow, etc. The friendliest dogs generally are mixed breeds. Then there are those you just can't judge. Environment has a lot to do with dog disposition too. The proverbial "junkyard" dog is one to be avoided! Mostly, the smallest of "house dogs" can be the biggest nuisance. They will bite much quicker than a big dog, especially if they are in the presence of their owner. Evidently, they must feel protected from counter attack when their owner is present. In fact, the only time I was ever bitten was by a small dog when the owner was standing right beside me. I wanted to ring her neck.....the woman, not the dog!

I remember a farm dog once that "scared my mule" as an old boss of mine used to say. I was looking for a rural customer way out in the country who had reported telephone trouble. There were seldom any addresses or box numbers; so, very often, it was necessary to stop and ask for directions. I had stopped at an old farmhouse, parked my truck at the bottom of the hill and began walking up towards the house. When I was about 30 feet from the house, a big dark brown hound dog eased his way around the corner of the porch and walked toward me. He didn't think I belonged there and seemed a little unsure what he should do about it. He didn't bark, but rather just nosed my pants leg enough to cause me to stop in my tracks. He had a look about him such that if I made one wrong move, he'd eat me alive! While he deliberated the situation, he wanted me to stand still. When I made the slightest move, he'd nose my leg again like he was getting ready to bite. Usually, I was able to talk calmly to a dog and carefully try to pat his head and make friends. It was different with this one! I simply did not know what to do; but I reasoned that I had better try to get back to the truck before the dog had any more time to think about it. So, I began taking small steps (in spite of the dog nosing me on the leg). After what seemed a long distance, I had worked my way almost back to the truck. Then, I reached down to my tool pouch, grabbed a roll of friction tape and threw it so the dog could see where it landed. He wasn't about to fall for that old trick and run after it, however, it did catch him by surprise long enough to allow me to jump in the truck. The quickness of my last move caused him to realize he had allowed a trespasser to escape and he was not happy! The paint on my truck door was never the same from his paw marks. That was the nearest I ever came to getting eaten alive by a vicious dog.

Bill Meeks had a good "cat" story. He was stringing drop wire for a new service. At that time, it was not uncommon to string two rolls of drop for one customer.....that would be 2400 feet. It was called "stretching a wire up a holler' where I came from. Anyway, as Bill was pulling the wire along the roadside, he came across a woman standing in her from yard. She was looking up at a large tree and sobbing like a baby. Bill approached her to ask about her problem. "It's my cat. It's stuck up in this tree and can't get down." Bill looked up and saw the cat. It was about 20 feet up. He already had his hooks on and he wanted to be of help; so, Bill started up the tree. Upon reaching the cat, he grabbed it and stuck it into his ditty bag hanging from his belt. The cat had other ideas on that matter. It jumped out of the bag, onto Bill's shoulder and dug his claws firmly into Bill's skin. Being a cool-headed type, Bill just climbed down with the cat clinging to his skin and drawing blood the whole way down. Once back on the ground, Bill and the woman struggled to get the cat to release his claws after which Bill said, "I let out a rebel yell heard clear back at the work center!' Afterward, he said, "Well, that was my good deed for the day!"

Ralph Teal (old power company lineman and friend) had a dog story (so to speak). Ralph was working in an alley rearranging some drop wires. He was by himself so doing the job in a safe manner required extra care and time. It was a tedious job and Ralph had been working at it for several hours. Of course, the neighborhood dogs barked constantly for the first hour and then tapered off when they realized he was not going anywhere. At one point, Ralph had to step inside a fence in order to pick up one drop he had previously lowered from the pole.

All of a sudden, something was on his back scratching and clawing! Ralph's first thought was a dog or a big cat had jumped him. Low and behold, it was a bantam rooster protecting his territory. Finally seeing the thing, Ralph swung around and swatted at it, knocking it to the ground. Then, with his size 14 Lineman's boot, he kicked it from one end of the yard to the other. Ralph said later, he never saw the feisty rooster again!

Another dog incident happened when I was once again working out in the country. I had an installation order for new service. The lady of the house showed me where she wanted the phone and I began working. It was a small one-story frame house built up on a concrete block foundation. I drilled a hole through the floor stuck the station wire through the hole, running several feet down through to make it as visible as possible from the crawl space. Next, I grabbed some "drive rings" and a hammer and began crawling under the house. I spotted the station wire way across on the other side from the crawl space opening (naturally). After making my way on hands and knees to the wire, I grabbed it, coiled it up and threw it towards the opening where the protector (point of termination) was located. As I threw the wire, I heard something from one of the dark corners of the crawl space. Shinning my flashlight around, I spotted a dog. He was a good-sized, short-haired Heinz “57". I called to him at first, but then realized there was something wrong with him. He was foaming around the mouth, which is a typical indication of a rabid condition. He didn't seem to have any inclination to move or come toward me, so I made my way back over to the crawl space opening, pulling the wire with me.

"Please Harry, not over my Princess® Phone!"

After I got out from under the house, I went to the kitchen door and told the lady about the dog under her house. Nonchalantly, she said, "Oh yeah, that dog went under there yesterday. I think he's mad." "What!" I said. "You let me crawl under there knowing about the mad dog under there?" "Well," she said, "I just forgot."

Oh brother, I wanted tell her off, pick up my tools and get out of there. But, I didn't! She got her service installed that day, and I learned another lesson about weird people!

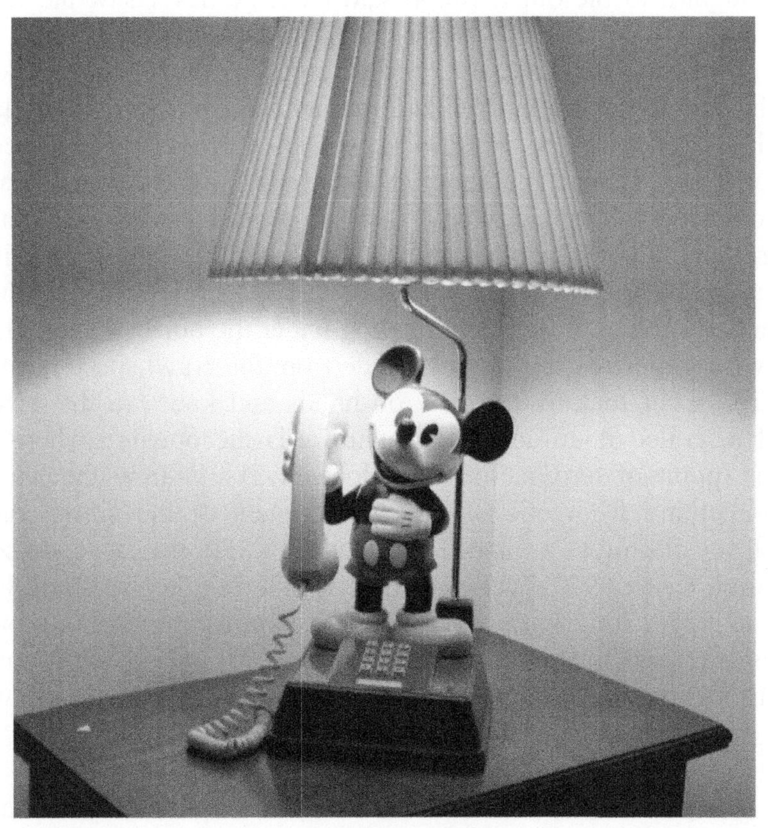

A prized possession….and it still works!

CHAPTER 15 - ENGINEERING

For a number of years, I had the good fortune of working as an Outside Plant Engineer. After twelve years as a craftsman, I got called into the District Engineer's office and was offered the job by the DE, Dick Snelling. My degree was in business and I never had aspirations in the direction of engineering. As it turned out, it was a good move and I loved it!

<Not this kind, the telephone kind…

I thought I knew outside plant pretty well, but actually had no idea how much I didn't know until the engineering job. In retrospect, I believe the best lesson of engineering is simply the discipline. In designing a job, everything that winds up on the drawing is there for a specific reason….no more, no less. My first Supervising Engineer, Harold Orum, required that I quote "chapter and verse" from the BSPs or other source as to the way I had done every job. He was the best teacher I ever had.

One of the most satisfying things about the engineering title is the respect shown by others. After gaining some amount of experience and the right training as described above, an engineer could justify his job to construction people with little or no argument. I hasten to add at this point that a good construction man and/or splicer could make or break an engineer, depending upon his degree of cooperation. It had to be a team effort to work right. Unfortunately, the District Level Managers sometimes made the cross-departmental cooperation a very tight rope to walk. Often, it was their ego and not common sense that took precedence.

One of my first assignments as a new engineer was a "down anchor" removal job. After making a field trip to the location, I drew up the job and gave it to my supervisor. Little did I know I had been "set up"! It seems the anchor removal job was routinely given to new engineers. The multiple anchors to be removed were located in the side yard of the District Engineer. There were about six of them and each was there for a specific purpose (according to the BSPs). Removal had been explored many times by many different engineers, but could not be done without violating established guidelines. Naturally, my proposed job did not get beyond my supervisor. Rather, he called a meeting of all the engineers, displayed my job on an easel and proceeded to demonstrate why it was not correct and if completed would be in violation of the "practices". Actually, it was all done in fun; i.e. not to embarrass me, but to enjoy the humor of the thing that all of the others had been through when they were new to the job. It was sort of like an "initiation" to a fraternity.

About 1970, the Company introduced an outside plant design plan known as Serving Area Concept (SAC). It was a departure from "Dedicated Plant" because "distribution" pairs were dedicated instead of "feeder" pairs. My good friend, Ed Ellie, was the 2nd level Plant Manager in Titusville. He had a "dedicated" area that was set up and managed correctly from the start. He saw to it! When SAC was introduced and his dedicated area was incorporated into a new SAC area, Ed was not happy. He had his hands full with "held orders" about everywhere except his dedicated area and he didn't want that disturbed. Now when a certain new engineer designed a job to use his dedicated feeder pairs to serve a much larger new SAC area, old Ed pitched a fit. Alas, it was a losing battle for him. The SAC concept had support all the way down from company headquarters and it was a good one! And, it didn't take long for Ed to appreciate it as well. SAC is still in use and earning its stars every day.

Another SAC related story comes to mind. We had an area in our beach community that was at about 98 percent fill. That's when 98 percent of the available cable pairs are in use and only two percent are left for new service. It was just a matter of time before having to deny service to new customers, a thing we just couldn't tolerate in those days. The only solution was to establish a new SAC area and bring some new feeder pairs out of the underground (conduit) to serve it. There was one big problem. The conduit was in the middle of the median of a heavily traveled road. Not only that, there were numerous government and special service cables under the pavement. I set up an "on site" meeting with the Contract Foreman, Richard "Speed" Tufts, to get his opinion and to explain the urgency of the job. Speed recognized the hazards of drilling under the pavement in the presence of all the other cables, but agreed to give it a shot. I drew up the job and submitted it to Construction. A few days later, we got a call from the Division Construction Office that they were not going to do the job. It was too hazardous to the existing buried cables. We, of course, alerted our Division Engineer, who agreed to come down from the Division Offices to have a look. This young engineer's knees were knocking, but nevertheless got ready to present his case. As it turned out, the Division Engineer, whom everyone feared greatly, did almost all of the talking and sold himself on the need to proceed with the job.

The day arrived when the Contractor crews were to start the job. The state road permit had been approved, the other utilities had been notified, the cables had been "located" and the drilling had begun. It wasn't long before the drilling was much too close to the government cables. The contractor crews were nervous, the contract foreman was nervous, and I was nervous. Thoughts of stopping the job were felt by all involved, yet the work proceeded. Finally, the drilling hit the side of the manhole in the middle of the median. What a relief! The new cable was placed and the SAC area was established for the much needed facility relief. But, in the process, I lost the friendship of my friend, Speed. Could it have been done another way? In retrospect, I still don't think so. However, I should have tried harder to get full commitment from Construction before starting the job.

The nature of the job and the strong desire to provide Bell System quality service commonly caused a lot of friction with co-workers. That's what made the "Breakup" so distasteful. A lot of good telephone people gave their hearts and sometimes their friendships to provide the best service in the world. When divestiture came along, there seemed to be very little support from our customers. I guess they bought the notion their telephone bills would be reduced. Maybe they had paid their phone bills all their lives and just wanted to see how it would be with competition present.

The above SAC story reminds me of another young engineer who was facing a perplexing day. Don Rice had been given the assignment of presenting the SAC concept to a group of engineers in another town. He was competent enough on the subject, but speaking before a group was not his cup of tea. On the day of the meeting and just prior to his speech, he went into an adjacent room and was pacing the floor. The District Engineer's Clerk, Hazel Right, happened by and asked him, "Don, are you nervous?" Don, protective of his image, said, "No, why do you ask?" "Well" said Hazel, "you're in the Ladies Restroom!"

State road permits were always a hassle. The State was very particular about what they wanted to see on the permit application. Invariably, there was always an engineer who thought he could submit a "slack" permit, and get it approved. One such guy was Bill Barnes. He was down-right incompetent in about all areas. After several attempts to get approval for a new cable under an interstate highway, he finally gave up. He didn't last long in our office and wound up going back to the town from which he came. After he had been gone for several months, we learned he had talked a contractor crew into placing his new cable in a storm drainpipe beneath the interstate highway, needless to say a forbidden act. At that point, the cable had long since been "turned up" and was serving quite a few customers. We chose to ignore it, although I must admit I lost some sleep wondering how we would serve the area if the State ever required us to remove Bill's cable from the drainpipe. Fortunately, I was transferred to another town and never had to worry about it again.

Railroad permits were even worse. They were extremely difficult to get approved. The railroads were there first and they used that fact to exercise their authority over their rights-of-way. They required thirty feet of clearance. Recall, normal road clearance was eighteen feet. Thirty feet was sometimes very hard to get. In fact, it almost always required unusually tall poles on each side. After many hours of preparation and follow up questions, Engineer Ed Rutherford finally got his approved. On the day of construction, Ed went out to the site to watch the line crew in their work. He in fact took his measuring stick (a long pole in several sections which can be extended to measure heights) so he could make sure there was at least thirty feet of clearance. After the new poles were placed and cable was hoisted up, properly sagged and secured at the through-bolt, Ed put up his stick and satisfied himself that he indeed had his thirty feet and then some! About the time he was lowering his stick and still discussing the remainder of the job with the construction foreman, a railroad truck pulled up. The railroad employee got out, looked at the new poles. Then he asked Ed why they had gone to the trouble of getting that much clearance when the railroad had just decided to abandon that section of their track. Ed was furious! These many years later and long after the track has been removed, I'm sure most people who drive by that area must wonder what those big, high poles are doing there for no apparent reason.

When I was in Engineering, each engineer had a territory and was responsible for both feeder and distribution facilities. Later, they divided the job responsibilities into planning, feeder, distribution, etc. and introduced corresponding titles. But, in the good old days as they say, an engineer did it all from the "tip" cable off the frame to the distribution terminal at the house and everything in between. It was sort of like how football used to be when each guy played offense, defense and special team.

One Supervising Engineer for whom I worked was Harry McElveen. He was a Georgia Tech graduate, a really smart guy and I liked him. After Georgia Tech, Harry had gone into the army and later hired by the phone company upon completion of his duty. He had no experience with telephone outside plant, but he was a quick learner. He and I went out to check on some conduit that Construction said could not be pulled. It apparently had some kind of obstruction and the linemen had given up on it. However, it was of such importance that we had to see for ourselves. So, Harry and I took a surveyor's "chain" to "fish" the conduit because it was longer than the standard Fish Tape. Harry didn't have any experience with fishing conduit, but he was not one to be overshadowed in any situation. Thus, before tackling the conduit fishing job, Harry asked if I could "throw a chain" (a surveyor's term for unwinding a coiled up chain). I should mention that the term "chain" refers to a flat, solid steel strand of wire, very similar to a standard electrician's Fish Tape. It is not a chain in the normal sense of the word. Harry had to "bring me along" that day because I had never "thrown a chain". Of course, he demonstrated the technique like a professional instructor. I imagine he had learned to do it perhaps in a surveying class at Georgia Tech. I acted as the “laborer” that day and used the “chain” to fish the conduit. Luckily, I got it through and Harry felt he had contributed. Also, he felt he had done his supervisor's duty with the training exercise of "throwing a chain". As I always said, a day without learning something new is a day wasted! Harry may have learned a little about fishing conduit that day too!

Warren Blanks was an outstanding engineer and a fine southern gentleman. He had the reputation of being able to take the neatest, most comprehensive notes of anyone. He was an artist! His field notes were so complete and perfectly legible they could have been printed and sent to Construction without any help from the drafting clerks. He had a curious side though and it occasionally got him in trouble. Warren could not pass by a closed box or paper bag without opening it to look inside. Our engineering office was the typical "bullpen" (one big room) with desks and drafting tables and a walkway through the middle. Warren's desk was in the back, which meant he had to pass by every other desk and table to get to his. After lunch, people would commonly come back with a package they had purchased and leave it on the edge of their desk. Warren could not resist opening each one to peek inside.

One day, fellow engineer Ben Pierce set a trap for Warren. After lunch, Ben placed a paper bag full of dog dung on a table near the front of the office. Sure enough, Warren came strolling by and opened the bag. He looked in, looked around the room to see who might be looking at him, looked in the bag again, and even leaned over to smell it. Very quickly, he stood back up, folded the bag top and walked to his desk mumbling something like, "Smart alecks! Funny! Really funny!"

In the category of “Most Embarrassing moments”, the day rolled around when I had to meet the Division Engineer about a job I had submitted. He had reviewed it and did not like it! Needless to say, we were all terrified of him! I wasn’t even sure what he liked or did not like, but I anticipated a “drumming down”. My Supervising Engineer as well as the District Engineer naturally wanted to go along for the ride. They had approved of my job so they were on the hook right along with me. One last visit to the Men’s Room and we would be off. I looked in the mirror to make one last appearance check. Recall we wore suits and ties in those days. As bad luck would have it, I must have ground my teeth in some off-center way. Next thing I knew, I was catching one of my very front teeth that had just fallen off my partial denture. Oh no! How could I face the boss's, boss's boss with a missing front tooth? I tried to stick it back in place, but it wouldn't stick. It just sat there! If I moved my mouth the least little bit, it would fall out again. I had no choice.....I had to keep the appointment! The good Lord was watching over me that day. When we got to the job site, the big boss was there. He had gotten there quite early and had already satisfied himself that the job was correct and needed. I didn't have to say a word and kept my mouth shut. My boss knew I was extremely white-knuckled that day, but he figured it was about the job. He never found out about the real reason.

As a part of the engineering job in the Cape Kennedy area, it was necessary to have a U.S. Government "Secret" security clearance. If you have ever applied for one, you know of the detailed application required. The government goes to great length in their background check before issuing the badge. Once obtained, I had almost complete access to all property on the Cape. It was a nice perk which I enjoyed very much, especially on days when they were launching a missile. A ring-side seat to those spectacular shots was worth a small fortune. Later, after leaving the area, I was required to relinquish my clearance badge. The debriefing that Uncle Sam put me through was worse than the original effort to get the thing in the first place! Makes me wonder how undesirable people ever get inside our country and how they manage to stay here! Maybe they have relaxed the standards (or lack thereof) the same way telephone service has gone over the past 20 years!

Before leaving the subject of security, I recall an incident that made me scratch my head and roll my eyes. It happened near the Cape during the early space years. Once again, let me emphasize the time frame, location and the extremely strong security. Recall, our country was in a race to space with the Soviets and they took security very seriously. As is common on government sites, they owned and maintained all of their plant facilities. In other words, their facilities were isolated to the outside world until cross-connected at an interface point. We referred to it as the Tip Shack. It was a small, remotely located concrete building on the property limits of the Cape. It contained a cross-connect frame with government cables terminated on one side and our cables on the other. When required, we would go into the building and run jumpers to establish whatever connect-through service the government wanted. The outside door of the building was made of heavy metal and equipped with an elaborate combination lock. It was probably not as secure as a bank vault, but nonetheless very secure! The first time I had to go into the Tip Shack, I had to ask not only about how to find it, but also how to get in once I was there. The Installation Foreman told me to give him a call when it came time to go out and he would meet me there. In the meantime, I was taking a break with a fellow installer and I mentioned about having to go to the Tip Shack. He said, "Judge, you don't need the Foreman. Just go on out there....the combination is written on the outside wall right beside the door." So much for security! Sure enough, when I got there and walked up to the door, it was indeed written in plain sight for anyone to see! Well, that was many years......before 9-11, airport security checks, drug testing, roadside bombs and the like! As far as I know, there were never any security breaches at the Tip Shack!

Another interesting day developed while very far out from the office and in the opposite direction from the Cape, I was driving down a narrow, one-lane sand road on a very large, private cattle ranch in Central Florida. I was in my Bell System green car with the gold Southern Bell decal on the door. I had my Company ID, my Secret security clearance badge and my shiny white hard-hat with "Engineer" on the front. With those items along with my exaggerated feelings of self importance, I could go almost anywhere. Actually, I was driving toward the well fields that supplied water to my town. We had a few circuits of open wire used for telephone and monitoring of water pressure. And, we had constant complaints from the water department that they couldn't hear on their telephones. The problem was well known in our office. It was due to transmission problems with the extra long loop from the office. Somehow, my predecessors had successfully put off doing anything about the problem. Unfortunately, I was not so lucky! Down the road ahead, I could see a cloud of dust coming toward me. Moments later, a very dusty pickup truck came straight down the middle of the road heading right for me! There was a little room to pass on the narrow road, but this guy wasn't moving over! He was right smack in the middle. I had no choice but to stop! Then the door of the truck opened and the driver got out. He was a very big, burly cowboy-looking character who upon stepping foot on the ground, pulled his side pistol and asked me what I was doing there. Good grief! I asked him why in heck he couldn't see my Bell-System green car with the gold Bell-System emblem on the door. He didn't crack a smile. He just said they had problems with cattle rustlers and was making sure who I was. With that, he got in his truck, backed up quite a long way to a turn-around and headed back in the direction from which he'd come. I had a notion to turn around myself and not do anything to improve the service, but that old Bell System service ethic kicked in and I continued on my way. Later, the job was completed for some remote amplifiers which fixed the transmission problem. And, I learned a little about self-importance and humility from the cowboy! All in a day's work, huh!

A somewhat similar story was related to me by Carl Taylor, an old lineman friend and safety foreman with Florida Power Company. Several line crews had a pole setting and transfer job just off an interstate highway. The only access to the pole line was through a very large privately owned orange grove. Prior to starting the job, permission was obtained and arrangements were made to enter through a gate so the crews could drive through the grove to the work location. The day rolled around to do the job, but the crews found the gate locked. There were several trucks and a good sized crew of men. Time and money were wasting! So, they decided to bust the lock and go on through to the job. Rather than leave the gate unlocked, Carl placed a lock of his own back on the gate. By noon time, the grove owner and a few of his men decided to check on the power crews, but discovered the new lock on the gate. He was locked out of his own property! He was furious that he couldn't get into his own property! At that point, he busted Carl's lock and placed another lock of his own back on the gate. And, with that, he told his men to go after Carl and bring him to his office. Reluctantly, Carl pulled off the job and went to see the guy, who proceeded to dress down Carl with a barrage of cussing commonly attributed to sailors. Carl let him blow off his steam and apologized for the busted lock. Then Carl calmly informed him that he owed him $10 for the lock he busted. The guy was shocked for a moment, but then burst out in laughter....and Carl joined in. The incident ended with no further problems and no further stand-offs. Before the job was completed, the grove owner provided the line crews with a ranch-style barbeque fit for kings.

During my tenure in Engineering, our office got a new District Engineer by the name of Bob Ringstrand, certainly an appropriate name for a telephone employee to say the least! Mr. Ring (as I called him) transferred in from the North and quickly turned our office upside down. He was a P.E. (Professional Engineer) and smart in many ways, but had little time for traditional southern social graces. His first responsibility must have been to firmly establish who was boss as he turned down almost every job that hit his office. Surely he wanted us to fully understand that he ran the show! He also loved to needle the District Plant Manager and the District Construction Supervisor. They had weekly meetings to determine which jobs would be started. The constant shortage of MCF (cable) and money provided the perfect platform for argument, bickering and table pounding among the three. I was assigned to take on the job of scheduling for our department. My counterpart in Construction was Wayne Crawford. After attending several of the weekly meetings and having to sit through the very tense atmosphere, Wayne and I got together with a plan. Prior to the meeting we called one another and planned our strategy. We discussed the jobs that he felt he needed and those I felt we needed. Then we decided which ones we could work given the cable and money we had available. When we got to the meeting, Wayne would bring up his jobs and I would bring up mine. Each of us would debate the pros and cons of our jobs just as we had rehearsed by phone and eventually agree on the ones to be done. They, of course, were the jobs we had already agreed on before the meeting. The district managers were satisfied each had stood his ground and fulfilled his duties. Meetings got a lot smoother from then on. And, by the way, Mr. Ring turned out to be a very good boss. I left the Engineering Department soon afterward, but have always second-guessed my leaving. I could have benefited greatly from more of Mr. Ring's experience and counsel.

One of best preparations for Engineering was experience in Plant Assignment. That was the first destination for a service order after the initial customer contact with the business office. The job was inside, clean, cool in the summer and warm in the winter and interesting. It was my job to receive the service orders for the day, assign a telephone number, cable pair, and terminal number. Then the service orders were grouped according to general location and assigned to each IR for the next day. For our cable records, we used the old, trusted Acme binders. With that background, I was able to bypass that part of the usual learning curve of the rookie Engineer.

One of the first engineering assignments for most was working held orders, a term given to a service orders that could not worked due to the lack of plant facilities. A "held order" meant that a customer had requested service, but could not get it for one reason or another. Usually it was due to the lack of a vacant cable pair or existing plant altogether. Once determined, it often led to a job order for placing new cable or a new terminal. Sometimes, we could make a cable throw. Two separate cables having the same cable designation and pair count was common in those days. It was called Bridge Tap. As more facilities were placed, it became common practice to remove bridge tap. Prior to that time, a cable throw could very often provide relief by changing the count of one cable "leg" or a terminal. Experience with the old Acme Cable Records would reveal to the trained eye the best way to do the throw. A lot of new Engineers were embarrassed by a splicer or assignor when the throw didn't go well. There are few things more humiliating to an engineer than getting a call from a cable foreman or assignment foreman that a cable throw had to be stopped because of the lack of vacant cable pairs.

Probably the most diverse assignment given to engineers was "security duty" during a strike. They actually sent us to school to learn the proper technique of recording statements, taking depositions, documenting evidence, etc. Each engineer was assigned a location to provide escort service for the female employees from the building to their cars. We didn't carry guns or clubs; we just had the job of walking the pretty girls to their cars.....tough duty! The first day of the strike, I was sitting in the District Marketing Manager's office, my assigned post for the day. He had an absolutely gorgeous secretary who was known to wear very short skirts, common in the 1970s. I was on the phone talking with Bill Craft back in the Engineering Office. Bill had worked this post the day before. During our conversation, the short-skirted secretary walked in and leaned over the desk opposite mine. She had her back to me and left little to the imagination regarding her back side. I was so taken by the moment that I could not even speak. Bill said, "What's the matter? Did Michelle walk by?" A long moment later, I said, "It's worse than that!" Bill laughed and said, "Oh, she must have bent over the desk in front of you!"

Speaking of security duty, Amber Jaynes, CADD Operator and good Pioneer friend, recalled a bomb scare in our main C.O. during the 1996 Olympics. The Company had placed razor wire on the fence around the building and even welded the manhole covers shut. They were serious about security and wanted the whole world to witness. Well, on this particular morning, a supervisor found a mysterious box at the front door. Everyone was ordered to evacuate the building. The police were called who in turn called out the GBI (Georgia's equivalent to the FBI). Then a bomb squad was called in to check out the mysterious box. Everyone was anxiously watching from an adjacent parking lot across the street....exciting stuff! The bomb squad placed sand bags around the box and somehow got a rope around it as well. Then they began pulling the box away from the door and out into the street to their detonation device. The box was eventually opened. It was not a bomb at all! Rather, it merely contained someone's lunch along with a note. The note was as follows: Hi Honey: I put in some "Texas Pete" for your sandwich today. That ought to give you a big bang, but if it gives you heartburn, don't blame me! Amber said, "Thank goodness, it didn't give us a big bang, but needless to say, it gave everybody heartburn that day!"

Earlier, I mentioned Harry McElveen, my good friend and supervising engineer. He was promoted several times and eventually wound up a vice president at company headquarters. A funny thing happened along the way while working in the Cape area. Dick Snelling was District Engineer at the time and insisted everyone in the Engineer Department belong to the local chapter of IEEE, International Electrical and Electronic Engineers. The local college owned a 90 foot yacht which IEEE used for meetings (entertainment). And, Dick volunteered our group for the job of tending the lines while it was docked at Cape Canaveral. Harry decided to make a family thing of it and invited his wife and two children to spend the night on the boat. I was assigned to relieve them the next morning. When I arrived the morning after, they were all green and seasick. Why they just didn't get off the boat and sit on the dock, I'll never know. In any event, they were glad to see me, but immediately got in their car and went home.

The Engineering Department was a great learning experience that prepared me for the remaining sixteen years of my working days. Of the many different jobs I had over the years, it was not my favorite, although I think it would be a close second. It was sometimes a matter of "one- upsmanship". My BS degree didn't get full respect by the "Double Es", but I always felt my plant experience tended to provide a worthwhile balance between textbook engineering and the practical needs of the outside workers. In any event, it was a great seven years that I wouldn't have missed for the world!

Here's a napkin from Mr. B's in Ames, Iowa, home of Iowa State University. Whew! This was a wild place! They started "lap-dancing" there before the term had even been coined!

Remember the Sheldon-Munn Hotel? If you know about these two places, chances are you attended Advanced Engineering Economics at Iowa State University.

One more thought while on engineering. Recall, much of the space program was put together by the corporate world. Names such as Boeing, Pan Am, Bendix, RCA, GE, Rockwell, Grumman, etc. worked as partners with NASA and the military. Thus, thousands of common working class folks became an important part of the space program. And, a few really good telephone men and women worked on it as well. A few such "superstars" who come to mind (some already mentioned in a story) were Dick Snelling, Bob Ringstrand, Harold Orum, Harold Downing, Harry Mc Elveen, Gordon Titus, Warren Blanks, Ben Pierce, Bill Craft, Ed Rutherford, Jean Belec, Doris Knott, Terri Walters, Rita Cowart, Bob Weir, Wayne Crawford, John Vandergrift, "Bama" Mathews, and the list could go on….all of Cocoa, FL. Many thanks should go to them and all the other good, hard working telephone family of folks who were so dedicated to Ma Bell and to the space effort.

SOUTHERN BELL TELEPHONE AND TELEGRAPH COMPANY
Subject: Plan a "head"

Mr. Jerry Potts
P.0. Box 1887
Cocoa, Florida

Dear Sir:

It has come to our attention that you are planning toilets for your new building at 123 Play Knoll Avenue in Cocoa, Florida. We will be happy to assist in planning or reviewing your floor duct layout.

If you will provide us with preliminary building and “plop” plans showing proposed seating arrangements, we will return them to you indicating a satisfactory system or concurrence with your proposed system.

We would appreciate hearing from you. Our engineer, Miss Lucie Bowels, can be reached by calling Prunes 5-4321.

Yours truly,

Supervising Engineer (Engineers love to play around too.)

CHAPTER 16 – HEADQUARTERS

With 19 years of Plant and Engineering experience and eight long years of (night) college, I was promoted to company headquarters. My mail was now addressed "Dear Executive". No more shirt and tie without the coat. A three-piece suit was more the order of the day. Now the young ladies are holding doors open for me. No more 8 to 5 now it's 8:30 to 5. No more "bullpen" desk with little privacy; now it's a cubicle with walls (well almost). Wait! Let me pinch myself, after all I'm just an old telephone man!

Bellsouth HQ-Atlanta, GA (Now AT&T, but up for sale)

When I got to headquarters, I'm sure I felt like the Avon Lady who knocked on a door and was greeted by Tammy Faye Baker. I was excited about the opportunity! I had my Degree in Business Management and I was eager about the prospects of sharing my knowledge with the "big boys". No one ever told me that they might not want to listen. I think I found that out the first day I arrived there.

I was asked to go "upstairs" to meet with the assistant vice president to discuss my new assignment. I entered his office and began "sharing" with him some of my "expertise". He listened quietly for about two minutes; then he said, "Sit down, and let me tell you about the deck I'm building on the back of my house". I learned a valuable lesson that day on southern social graces in the workplace.

My first headquarters boss was General Thomas H. Norman, a Brigadier General in the Air National Guard. He was a great boss and true southern gentleman.... without question the best boss I ever had. I owe him many things, not the least of which was my involvement in the Telephone Pioneers. He had so many pat phrases, such as "Some you win, some you lose and some get rained out". When he was surprised by something, he would say, "Whew! That scared my mule". In going to a meeting, he would say, "Don't worry, if they throw you out, I'll be outside to throw you back in". I think he was the originator of, "If it ain't broke, don't fix it". Before divestiture, he would say, "We can handle MCI. It's that new Mexican telephone company, Taco Bell that worries me!" Fortunately for him, Tom retired before divestiture. Just like Alexander G. Bell, he would have had great difficulty dealing with everything that came after him. Since the first edition of Just An Old Telephone Man, Tom has passed on. He and his wife, Margaret (or as he would say in his genuine southern fashion, his Bride, Miss Maagrut), contributed many, many volunteer hours with the USO at the Atlanta Airport. She continues even yet. Tom was working on his memoirs when he passed away. He titled it *How Sweet It Is*, one of his signature phrases. I have read the brief part that he had finished….it was a GREAT read. How unfortunate for all of us telephone folks that he did not get to finish it.

One thing I appreciated about working at headquarters was the high caliber of people. And, I hasten to add, there were some great managers in the field as well. But, generally the headquarters staff people were first class. Most were college educated and had good management skills. As with any organization, there were a few "bureaucrats" as well. By that I mean perpetual staff people who had never had a field job and were essentially "retired in place" to use an old engineering term for non-salvageable material.

When I arrived at headquarters, there were about 800 managers and about 700 clerical support people. My area of responsibility involved direct contact with about one hundred other managers, more or less. Work pressures were so acute that close friendships were difficult. That's where Pioneering played such an important role in providing the "Fellowship" portion of the original Pioneer tenets of Fellowship, Loyalty and Service. I recall a few individuals who were hard to work with on the job, but who were great friends at Pioneer social events. The modern-day companies apparently have lost sight of the value of fellowship away from the job… what a pity.

Another hindrance to close friendships was the somewhat unique (and counter-productive) phenomenon at headquarters called the "NIH" factor (Not Invented Here). Contrary to the "field" where there were constant job measurements (Indices) that tended to force cooperation toward common goals, things were different at headquarters. There was much more freedom which many used to promote their own goals and ambitions; therefore, the rivalries were fierce, both within the department and across departmental lines. However, the higher behavioral standards at headquarters tended to keep those rivalries somewhat in check.

A favorite headquarters phrase was "system wide". When making a decision involving costs, even a penny per item "system wide" would make a sizeable impact. Timing was critical too. If we were going before the Public Utility Commission for a rate increase, each day waiting for approval could mean millions in terms of "system-wide" as well as "company-wide" dollars.

Who Remember "Phone Centers"?

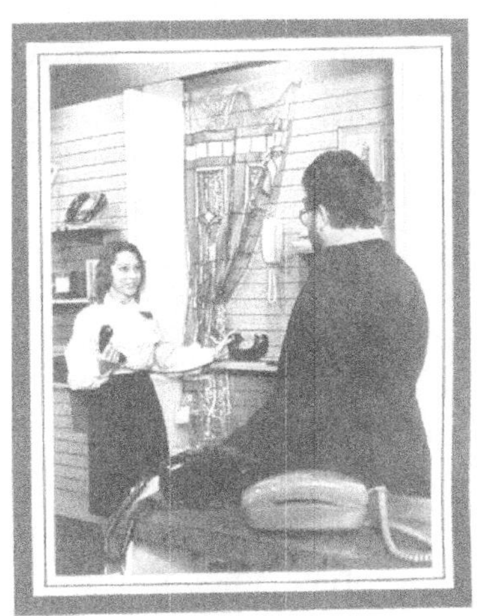

Phone Centers were Ma Bell's first experience with retail stores. They were often located in shopping centers. Initially, they sold "Design Line" telephones, long cords, etc. Later, cordless phones, answering machines, and eventually cell phones were sold. Having done some of the original cost studies on Design Line sets and aware of the slim margins of profit, I always wondered how those stores could justify their overhead. Design Line sales could not support that kind of overhead!

The answer was revealed when I reviewed a P&L (profit and loss) statement for these stores in one of our states. It seems they had failed to include the "cost of goods". It was like everything they sold was given to them at no cost. Naturally, profits looked pretty good! I tried to blow the whistle, but couldn't find anyone who wanted to listen. That and many other similar things led to the demise of "Ma Bell" (in my humble opinion)! Telephone sales went to AT&T at divestiture and, not surprisingly, it wasn't long before they closed the Phone Center Stores.

Mentioning Design Line telephones brings to mind another point. When they were introduced, Ma Bell maintained ownership of all equipment. Design Lines were the first things actually sold to the customer. However, the company retained ownership of the internal working parts to allow lifetime maintenance, which was customary with all equipment. It was a fantastic deal for the customer. There was a one-time charge for the "shell" and lifetime maintenance was provided at no additional charge. Now, nobody ever accused me of being smart (to quote a good telephone man and equipment engineer by the name of Fred Morris), but I knew there had to be a better way!

When I became involved with Design Line cost studies, other industries were already offering "maintenance contracts". They were not only selling their products, but were also selling maintenance as well. I recommended this to the "product teams" for Design Line phones, but, of course, the NIH factor came into play. Thus, nothing new ever originated at the company level, but rather always at Basking Ridge (AT&T Headquarters). After the appropriate amount of time had passed since the original suggestion, AT&T announced their new idea and Design Lines and Maintenance Contracts were sold. Consequently, Design Line phones finally became very profitable. Many other models were introduced after that and the whole line became a nice "cash cow" to use an overworked marketing term.

The big city and headquarters called for some adjustments. OK, I was a "kid in the big city"! And, I was still trying to get my bearings as I walked down Peachtree Street during lunchtime. I am admittedly a southern boy! I was raised with southern hospitality. If someone stops me on the street and wants to talk, I'll listen! Little did I know that it doesn't work that way in a big city! A panhandler stopped me on the street and told me he had some financial problems. He had a watch that he would let me have at an exceptional price if I could just help him out. The watch looked great and I was not one to pass up a good deal. It was a well-known brand with an upscale name. My initial reluctance to say OK worked to my advantage as he came down on his price several times during that first minute of conversation. I was no country bumpkin! I was a corporate executive! I would strike the deal to my liking or it would not get done. I was in control. The watch purchase was made and I went back to my office....whistling and happy! About an hour later, I noticed the watch had stopped! I opened up the back.......Made in Taiwan! Just one of many lessons to be learned the hard way!

Embarrassing moments....we've all had our share. Mario Soto, old friend and Florida U. engineer, had his one day while attending a departmental meeting. He was standing beside the Assistant Vice President, Mr. W.J.R Thomas, who was there speaking on the matter of the day. W.J.R. was a chain smoker. Mario was listening intently while also enjoying a piece of cake which was brought in for the meeting. Just as he put his fork to the next bite of cake, W.J.R. reached over and flicked his cigarette ashes in Mario's saucer. Mario's mouth dropped and remained open for a long, long, long-long minute! W.J.R. was not even aware of what he had done....and Mario or anyone else was not about to tell him!

Oh! Another moment of embarrassment came during a Telephone Pioneer event. Harold Hudlow, a fine southern gentleman and great Telephone Pioneer, was making his way through the crowd greeting each attendee in his usual friendly manner. Harold was a long-term employee who knew almost everyone in the company, at least he thought so. As he came to the next very distinguished looking guest, Harold said, "Hello, I'm Harold Hudlow. You look like you might have a bell-shaped head. Have we met?" "Well" said the guest "Well,

Harold, yes we have....I'm John Clendenin". Much to his surprise, Harold had failed to recognize the recently retired President and CEO of the company. Harold said afterwards it was like taking a scalding hot drink of coffee. Anything he said or did after that was going to be WRONG!

Back when I was coming up, most of the Company's top executives were truly great managers and true gentlemen. One such man was Bill Travis, senior executive vice president of Southern Bell. Today, the title for his position would probably be Chief Operating Officer or President. Mr. Travis ran the operations of the whole company. He was also the Jack Benny of the company, i.e. he not only watched every penny, but also was protective of his ultra-conservative reputation. Quite often, Bill worked Saturdays. On the day before, he would ask his secretary, Betty Wright McCowan (a fine southern lady and most professional secretary I ever knew) to call the building people and make sure the air conditioning was left on for the day. Not wanting people to know it was for his own comfort, he would ask her not to reveal who had called to request the A/C be left on. It was all about his image with the people he managed. He was concerned that people would consider air conditioning an extravagance! Some might say he was "old school", but it was that kind of stewardship (and example) that made the company so successful.

CHAPTER 17 - TELEPHONE SETS

As might be imagined, there have been a blue million different types of telephones used over the years. Shown below are a few of the most common ones, from earliest to latest. Some of the 500 type sets (with Touch Tone Pad) are still in use, but I doubt any of the others are. Western Electric was the largest manufacturer, but many were also made by Automatic Electric (later owned by General Telephone), Stromburg-Carlson, Gray and many others.

Old Magneto Wall Telephone

202 Type Wall Set

202 Non Dial Desk

"Workhorses" of the 20s and 30s

302 Desk Set

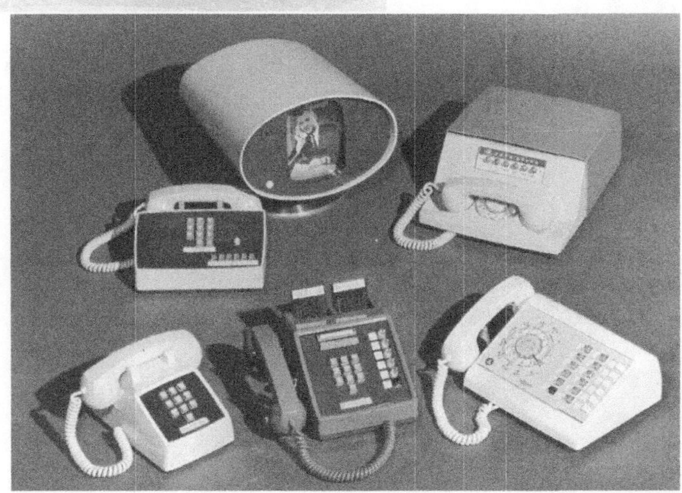

Front (l to r) 500 Type Touch Tone Desk, Card Dialer, Rotary Call Director Set
Back (l to r) Speaker Phone Key Set, Picture Phone, Data Set

Western Electric Manufacturing Plant, spun off from AT&T to become Lucent. Later they spun off to Alcatel (a French Telco). They have been "spinning" ever since...........or should I say spiraling"!

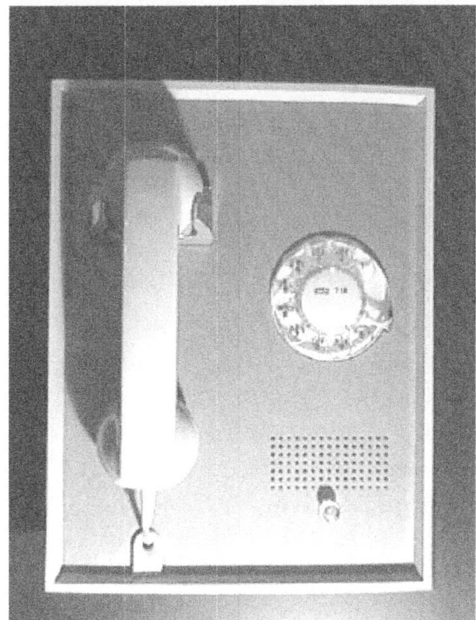

Remember this one? It's a Western Electric Model 750 Panel Telephone. It was a flush-mounted wall telephone set with retractable cord. It came out in the mid 60s, but never achieved great popularity due to the need for its pre-wired receptacle box in the wall. The knob on the front is a ringer volume adjustment.

The Panel Phone reminds me of another story. After a new home was pre-wired for these sets, covers were provided to hide the outlet box. These covers (or plates) were about nine inches by twelve and made of aluminum. They had a very attractive brushed finished much like today's newer stainless appliances. The obligatory Bell System

Logo was on the front. The story goes this way. One of our installers, who shall remain un-named, thought these covers would make a nice back-splash around the counter-tops of his kitchen at home. So, he began discreetly collecting enough covers to do his kitchen. His completed kitchen (I'm told) looked great, but he had forgotten all about the Three C's! Alas, he was found out and relieved of his job as well as the covers off the wall. Another good telephone man down the drain!

Bringing Universal Service to the farm -
Early 1950s

Recently, I had the good fortune of visiting the Georgia Rural Telephone Museum in Leslie, Georgia. Mr. Tommy Smith, owner, has assembled one of the largest collections of telephones and other related memorabilia in existence. I highly recommend a personal visit for hours of splendid viewing and reminiscing. Drive or catch the S.A.M. train near Cordele, just off I-75 south of Macon.

CHAPTER 18 - ALL IN A DAY'S WORK

So you want the day off! Let's take a look at what you are asking for. There are 365 days per year available for work. There are 52 weeks per year in which you already have two days off per week, leaving 261 days available for work. Since you spend 16 hours each day away from work, you have used up 170 days, leaving only 91 days available. You spend 30 minutes each day on coffee break that accounts for 23 days each year, leaving only 68 days available. With a one- hour lunch period each day, you have used up another 46 days, leaving only 22 days available for work. You normally spend 2 days per year on sick leave. This leaves you only 20 days available for work. We are off for 5 holidays per year, so your available working time is down to 15 days. We generously give you 14 day vacation per year which leaves only 1 day available for work so if you think you're going to get that day off forget it!!!!

Installation/Repair was such a fun job. It provided so many opportunities for a young rookie to go out into the world of work and begin the life-long journey toward old-age wisdom. Imagine a kid just out of high school. He goes into a perfect stranger's home with a service order and is confronted by a beautiful young girl with very few clothes making obvious advances. How does he deal with that having no prior experience? It's often said that experience is the best teacher. Rubbish! Experience lets you make the mistakes first before it teaches anything!

Once while working installation in a large apartment complex, I had an order with an incorrect apartment number. The apartment manager was so accustomed to seeing telephone men every day she would very readily hand out keys with little thought. This day, she handed me the key of the apartment number which was on my order. I found the apartment and proceeded to install the service. The next day, I had an order at the same complex and for the very same apartment number. It didn't take a lot of investigation with the manager to determine I had installed a phone in the wrong apartment and had closed the order! So, with the help of the manager, I did some rearranging and got each service in the right apartment. Our dispatcher was a sharp gal (I called her Dear Ann) and I'm sure she suspected something was amiss. I'm sure she knew there would be trouble if the first customer had made toll calls before I got the phones switched around. I had to lie to her that day and although I never heard any more about it, it has bugged me to this day!

Russell Pascal hired on as a Splicer's Helper. On his first day, his foreman drove him out to a worksite where some extended splicing work was ongoing. Recall in such a situation, splicers often drove their own cars to the site. Russell did all a rookie could do that first day to help the splicer. At the end of the day, the splicer went to his car and Russell went around and got in the passenger side. The splicer asked, "What are you doing?" Russell said, "Well, the foreman brought me out here and I don't have a way home." The splicer said, "Well, son, you're going to have to find a telephone and call him. I'm on my way home!" In the old days, there were few things lower than a new Splicer's Helper. And, the old splicers seldom did anything to make it any easier!

One day, I took a few minutes between jobs to go see a doctor. I had a cyst on my neck that had grown quite large and hard. The doctor took a look at it and told me it should come off. "I'll be over at the hospital at 2pm today." the doctor said. "Just go over there and report in at the "Out Patient" desk. They'll tell you what to do. It'll only take a few minutes." I said, "OK" and went back to work. Later, I went over to the hospital and found the out-patient office. I didn't know if I was supposed to walk right in or not, so I just stuck my head in. There was a big, woman nurse sitting there, looking like she did not want to be disturbed. I whispered, "Is Doctor Stiles in?" She whispered back, "No, come on in!" Before I could fully interpret her intentions, she handed my one of those little gowns that ties in the back (if you could reach back there). I said, "I'm only here to get a small cyst removed", pointing to the back of my neck. As if not even hearing what I had said, she told me to take my clothes off and put the

gown on. I may have argued more if she hadn't been twice my size and spoke with a 20-cycle wrestler's voice.

So, I got the gown on. Right away, I learned the meaning of term "ICU". She brought in a wheelchair and told me to sit down. I said, "I can still walk, you know!" as she shoved it up under me like a dog cold-nosing a cat's rear-end! Then she wheeled me out through the lobby (how embarrassing) and on to the elevator. When we got off, we were in the operating room. Everything and everybody was either covered in green sheets or wearing green clothing. They all had masks on and were scurrying around with IV bottles and more green sheets. I'm thinking, "Wait just a dad-burned minute! It's only a small cyst! There's been some mistake here. My little green truck is parked right outside! Just go to the window, you'll see!"

About that time, after moving me over on to an ice-cold table with wheels, my doctor came by. I could hardly recognize him under his greens and mask. I said, "Doc! What's going on here?" He said, "Just count backwards from 100." "One-hundred, ninety-nine, ninety-eight." I woke up later with a big bandage on my neck and the big nurse holding my hand. What a revolting ordeal! A little while later, I was back in my truck and on my way to the next job. I never went back to that stupid doctor again!

A doctor might have been needed one day if Alan Nobles had not been quick on his feet.....or was it his knees? Alan was a big guy....all man! He was built like a flower pot, i.e. the biggest, broadest shoulders you'll ever see, hard muscular arms, stout trim waist, and super strong legs. He was working under a house pulling wire through the crawl-space. He had made his way from the outside opening over to his wire. Just as he reached to grab it, he heard a dreaded sound.....rattle, rattle, rattle. Yes, it was a very large rattlesnake about three feet away. Alan later said it scared him to the point that he wanted to put his shoulders to a floor joist and raise that house right off the foundation. If anyone could have done such a thing, Alan could have done it! Fortunately he backed out safely (with the JK wire), the snake didn't attack and he got his service installed that day in spite of the frightening incident. It did take a little longer, however, due to an extended visit to a restroom!

My good friend Sam Templeton, a fine southern gentleman and cable splicer, was working in a manhole late one night splicing cable. Russell Pascal, fellow splicer and also fine southern gentleman, was working in the next manhole down the street. They both were wearing their headsets and communicating on a "talk pair". About 2AM, they both heard a horn honking somewhere from up top. At first, they paid little attention. It was common practice for other splicers to honk their horns as they drove by another splicer's work location. This time, however, the honking continued far longer than usual. Sam decided to go up to check it out. Upon reaching the top and sticking his head out of the manhole, he saw a strange lady in his truck honking the horn. By this time, Russell had also seen her and was on his way to find out what she was doing. When they got to the truck, it was obvious she was drunk as a skunk! She had already been in Sam's lunch box, ate his food, scattered paperwork all around and was sitting behind the wheel pretending to be driving and honking at traffic. They asked her to get out, but she refused. They told her they were going to call the police, but she told them she would "cry rape". After a short discussion between Sam and Russell, they got in the truck with her in the middle, drove down to the "red light" district and dumped her out on the sidewalk. For some reason, they just couldn't get back into the swing of splicing cable that night.

Jimmy McMullen was a fine southern gentleman and ace installer. He always made more than his share of "work units". Most thought it was because he was just a fast worker, but that was before we learned his secret. Usually, there is one best way to run an aerial drop from the terminal pole to the house. Near the point of attachment of the drop on the house, the protector and ground wire is installed. From that point, inside wire is then placed to the point of connection for the telephone instrument. The first question an installer asks a customer is where she wants the telephone. From that question, the installer can plan the rest of the job as to how he will run the inside wire. Sometimes, it might require five feet of wire to the protector and sometimes it might require a hundred feet of more. Jimmy's secret to fast installs and easy work units was his inside wire installations. He would tell the customer that inside wire only came is five-foot lengths. Thus, the telephone always wound up directly through the wall from the protector, a simple installation compared to the other installers placing long, labor intensive runs of inside wire.

Another story on Russell Pascal and Sam Templeton comes to mine. They were on loan and working out of town, staying at the Skyland Motel. After a hot day's work and a shower, they cleaned up to go out for dinner. Russell got dressed first and stepped outside his door for a smoke. About that time, an attractive young lady came out of her room next door. Russell introduced himself and turned on his best southern charm. In a few minutes, he talked her into going to dinner with him. Russell then asked her to go back in her room and wait until he came to get her. Meanwhile, Sam came out of his room and was ready to go. Russell told Sam that he wasn't feeling good and suggested he go on by himself. After Sam left, Russell knocked on the lady's door and asked if she was ready to go. Later at the restaurant, Russell and the lady were enjoying dinner when by coincidence Sam came strolling by their table. Before Russell could think of how to explain the situation, Sam greeted Russell and said, "Well hello Russell. By golly, it's good to see you! When did you get out? I thought you were in for life! And did your wife get alright after the attack?" By this time, the lady was looking for her purse and the nearest exit!

All installers carried a quarter inch by eighteen inch drill bit. It was sometimes called a JK bit and it had a small hole in the end for attaching wire. After drilling the hole, the wire could be threaded through the small hole of the bit and pulled back through the hole just drilled. That saved the installer the trouble and frustration of fishing the wire from one side of the wall or floor to the other. A typical inside wall is about five inches thick and consists of the two-by-four stud, drywall on each side and sometimes insulation. The drill bit above could drill through such a wall with a good twelve inches left over. On one otherwise uneventful day, James McCoy, one of the newer installers was running inside wire for a new install. He was stapling around the baseboard making his way to the kitchen. The last part of the run included going through an extra thick wall from a hallway into the kitchen and then up the wall to the telephone set location. James drilled the hole and wondered why the wall was so much thicker than normal, but paid no more attention to it. He drilled from the kitchen to the hallway, attached the wire through the little hole in his bit and pulled it back through. Then he stapled the wire up the wall to where he would mount the wall telephone set, a 554W-56 (a red 500 type wall set). He completed his order, signed it off with Dispatch and went on to his next order. Later that day, he was sent back to check on a problem the lady customer was having regarding her pocket door not working properly. It seems old James had drilled through a wall which contained a pocket door, the type that slides back into the wall rather than swinging on hinges. Of course, the wire ran right through the door and thus prevented it from moving more than an inch or so. James learned a valuable new installer lesson that day!

Another drill story of my own comes to mind. I had an order for an extension phone. The lady customer wanted it to sit on a small table near a very large and beautiful grand piano. I was a new, inexperienced installer at the time. The house had a basement and the protector was located there. Recall in the old days, drops were brought all the way into basements where a protector was mounted and a water-pipe ground was usually very close. Well, it was an easy run from the protector to the new phone location, but there were water pipes, gas pipes, electric wires, air ducts right where I wanted to drill down. So, I made several trips up and down the stairs to the basement measuring very carefully just where I needed to drill my hole for the inside wire. With brace and bit in hand, I methodically drilled the hole.....up from the basement....the exact wrong thing to do! After drilling the hole, I pushed the JK wire up through it and went upstairs to look for the wire. It was nowhere to be found. I took another look around the room and basement to verify the perspective. Surely the wire had to be there! I pulled the wire out, looked at the end to make sure it would go through the hole without hanging up. Back upstairs I went to look again for the wire, but it was not there! I was on my hands and knees, bending my head down to look all around when I noticed something unusual about one of the grand piano legs. The brass castor was resting on the floor, supporting the massive black leg of the piano, but there was a small, ivory-colored something running vertically from the floor, along-side the castor and up to the base of the leg. Oh good grief! If was my JK wire! I had drilled up and into the piano leg. Fortunately, the drill did not exit the leg and no harm was done except to make a nice nesting area for a hungry termite.

We all complained a lot about our bosses and most of us probably filed a grievance on occasion; but, imagine the training job they had to do with all the new kids. A green kid just out of high school thinks he knows it all when in reality he knows nothing! Whether it was a piano leg, busted plaster, personal injury or whatever, those first-level foremen had their work cut out for them. In retrospect, they did a pretty fantastic job.

A splicer's truck had a sizeable bed with toolboxes on each side. The bed was a little larger than a standard 1/2 ton pickup truck. It is important to understand the bed size to fully appreciate the next story. Back in the "good old days", a good many craftsmen had some kind of money making activity they could do in their off time; in other words, they "moonlighted". Recall from an earlier chapter, it was pointed out that Ma Bell did not pay as well as most people thought. The starting wage for an installer in 1955, for example, was $37.50 per week and not easy to live on! So, moonlighting was common. In those days employees with a farm upbringing were fairly common and this often led to their moonlighting activity. Fred Moore, cable splicer, raised a few cows and sold them at the farmer's market for a few extra bucks. Terry Sanford tells of being asked by Fred to go with him on a cable trouble. Instead of going to the trouble, Fred took him to a pasture and got Terry's help with loading a cow in the back of the splicer's truck. Then they took it to the market, sold it, and Fred pocketed the money. All the way to the market, Terry was watching for other "little green trucks" thinking they would be seen and reported for having a cow in a company truck. Terry didn't say how Fred explained the awful odor in his truck for several weeks afterward.

Fred and Terry’s story brings up another working team, PBX IRs by the name of Jerry Smith and Bob Stone. Bob was a little hard of hearing, yet he complained constantly of Jerry having that affliction. Jerry was considerably younger and had no such problem! One day while working in a doctor’s office, Bob decided he would ask the doctor how he could prove that Jerry was hard of hearing. The doctor told him to stand 15 feet behind Jerry and ask him a question in a normal tone of voice. If he did not answer, move closer to about 10 feet away and ask the same question. Then, if still no answer, move up to 5 feet away and try again. Later that day and back on the job, Bob saw

Jerry installing a wall set. So, he positioned himself 15 feet in back of him and said in his normal voice, “Jerry, what time is it?” He got no response! Bob moved to 10 feet back and asked the same question. Still no response from Jerry! Then Bob moved to 5 feet back and asked again, “Jerry, what time is it?” This time he heard Jerry say with some amount of irritation, “Good grief, Bob! For the third time, it’s three-thirty!” Alas, poor old Bob finally learned that day that he was the one with the hearing problem!

Calvin Thornberry was a three-year employee. He began as a lineman, but moved over to installer-repairman after about a year on the job. Cal was a tall, thin, good-looking young fellow who could always catch the young girl's eyes. Once while installing an extension for a cute, young housewife, Calvin got distracted and drilled down through a plastered bedroom ceiling. The plaster was soft and the drill only made a very small hole, but it was very visible. A frantic call to his foreman provided much needed relief. Cal had a habit of chewing gum, so his foreman told him to simply stick his gum in the hole. Then with some borrowed facial powder and a power puff, he dusted the gum with white powder. It was a first class repair job that was never noticed by the customer. Was it enough to cure Cal of his distractions by attractive female customers? I don't think so! He did, however, gain some respect for his foreman!

Kerwin Weeks, an old PBX IR, needed a wood burning stove for his newly converted porch to enclosed family room. After months of looking, he stumbled upon a good lead on one. While doing some rearranging of cable and key sets in a restaurant, he learned that the cook, an older black fellow, had left one in an old house that he had abandoned. He told Kerwin he could have it if he would go pick it up. After completing the job, Kerwin recruited the help of his friend, George Truman, and they went to get the stove. After some amount of searching for the address and the house, they finally came upon an old, dilapidated, wood-frame house. It did not appear lived in so they figured it must be the right house. The front door was locked so they checked the back door. It too was locked, but there was a simple wood latch that they were able to throw up and open the door. Upon entering, they noticed the wood stove sitting right there in the kitchen. After disconnecting the vent pipe, they were discussing the best way to move the thing when they heard a clock strike the hour. For a moment, neither knew what it meant. By the time they turned around to see the old wind-up wall clock, they had put two and two together and realized that if the house was abandoned, there was no way the clock could have been wound up. They were in the wrong house! Hurriedly, they put the vent pipe back on, locked the door back and escaped hoping they had not been seen. Kerwin went to the hardware store the next day and purchased a brand new wood burning stove for his new family room.

Aerial telephone cable was originally placed in pear-shaped rings on strand. For the uninformed, strand to the telephone business is spiral-wound, multi-wire steel cable such as found in bridge construction, guard-rails, guy wires, winches, and a million other uses. Telephone cable on the other hand is the lead or polyethylene covered "pipe" of small-gauge, multi-paired wire. The "strand" is placed from pole to pole first and then cable is lashed to that. Cable is attached to the strand by a device called a "lasher" unless self-supporting cable is placed (cable and strand both in the same sheath). But, in the old days, it was placed in rings, as mentioned above. I mention all of that for the benefit of the next story.

Ralph Nolan and Fred Benson, old cable splicers, were working on a "ringed" cable that ran very close to an apartment building. Splicers worked around the clock in those days and it was late one evening just before dark. Ralph began hearing female voices from an open window on the second story of the building. The cable was about even with the bottom of the windows, about 14 feet off the ground and about 18 inches from the side of the building. Curiosity got the best of old Ralph, so he stood up on the strand and hand-walked down the side of that building just to have a look in the window. Ralph thought he might get an eye full of girls in a compromising situation. Well, by the time he got to the window, they had left the room. Now Ralph had to get back, but he was unable to hand-walk in the opposite direction. Some things seem natural in one direction and unnatural in the other. That was the case that day and Ralph was stuck out on that strand and unable to get back to the pole. After much deliberation, he decided to continue in the same direction as he had started and make his way down to the next pole. The trouble came when he ran out of building and was still about 15 feet away from the next pole. Fred, still back at the other pole, climbed down, lowered his ladder, carried it down to the end of the building, raised it up to the strand and rescued poor old Ralph. They didn't even talk about it afterwards! I learned about it many years later and it is still just a funny.

Fred Sims had a trouble report at a farmhouse out from town. The subscriber complained of missed calls. She was on a multi-party line which, of course, required a good "ground". For that type of service, ringing current came in on either the ring side or the tip side of the line and went to ground. Ground was generally obtained with a ground wire from the protector to a strap attached to a cold-water metal pipe, a power company ground or a ground rod. This particular installation used a ground rod. Upon close inspection, Fred found that the ground rod had been placed horizontally just under the ground surface instead of being driven vertically straight down. The ground beside the house was very hard clay and the original installer took the easy way out to place his ground rod. In damp weather, the service would work fine, but when the ground dried out, the phone would not ring due to insufficient ground.

Actually, the hard clay and improperly placed ground rods were a fairly common problem and the subject of many odd....and hilarious stories. One such story involved a report of bells not ringing except at certain times. It seems the phone would ring only when the family dog urinated on the ground rod….or the housewife would throw out the washtub water on the ground rod! How funny is that! A variation of that tale had the dog chained to the ground rod and every time the phone rang, the poor old dog would let out a yell. Take your choice…..they're all possible…..and all funny!

Safety was Ma Bell's middle name! Actually, she had three....Quality, Quantity, and Safety! Safety was drilled into us on at least a weekly basis. There were regular safety meetings for the entire work force before beginning the workday. And, there were bumper meetings with your work group and foreman before leaving the work center. Then there were visits to the job by the foreman for an unscheduled truck inspection and safety check. We were always required to wear safety glasses while working…..few obeyed that one 100%. All trucks were equipped with "B" Voltage Testers which were used to check for foreign voltage on power ground wires, guy wires or whatever. But, in spite of everything done and said, there were many chances for something to go wrong and someone to be injured. Installer, Don Snyder, was walking along-side a road inspecting an open wire lead when a rock was thrown from a passing truck. It hit his left safety glass lens and cracked it like a spider web. The safety glass did not shatter as per design and Don saved his eyesight. He became a poster child for wearing safety glasses and his picture wearing the cracked glasses was plastered all over every work center in the company!

Another incident with potential dire consequences happened when Don Rice was using an electric drill to make a drop wire attachment on the facial board of a residence. He was on his step ladder reaching up with the drill in one hand. To give him leverage, he reached back to brace himself on a clothesline pole. Apparently, the drill was not properly grounded and the pole provided a very good path for the 120 volts to pass from the drill through Don's right arm, through the body and out the other arm to the pole. Afterwards, Don said if he had not been on the ladder, it could have killed him. He could not let go of anything, but fell from the ladder which pulled him away from the pole and caused him to drop the drill. He was shaken, but otherwise unhurt. I imagine most telephone people have a similar story and lived to tell about it. A few didn't!

Occasionally, a day would come up where service orders and trouble reports were light. We were encouraged to have a pet project where we could work and accomplish something worthwhile on slow days. One such project was the stepping of terminal poles. Terminal poles were climbed quite often and would get chewed up and splintered very quickly. On a slow day, we would find such a pole, strap on our tools, grab a bunch of pole steps and start up the pole. We always started with the highest steps (the two opposite one another) which were spaced so the terminal would be at chest level when safety'd off. Also, it was best to start at the top so we would not be working on hooks with steps below us. To cut out with steps below could be hazardous to say the least. I had nightmares about doing that and looking up from the ground to see my certain vital body parts hanging from a step. OUCH!

A brace and bit (that's a manually operated drilling tool to youngsters) was used to drill the hole, about 5/8 inches wide and about 5 inches deep. Drilling into a healthy 40 foot, class 5 Southern Pine Creosote pole is not an easy task, especially with a manually operated, now old-fashioned brace and bit! After the hole was drilled, the galvanized pole step was inserted into the hole. The step was threaded much like a very big screw or lag bolt. The lineman's hammer was used to hammer the step into the pole for a short distance. Then the hole in the hammer head could be used to turn the step in the rest of the way. The hammer handle provided quite a bit of leverage to turn the big step.

So, after completing the first two steps, you could take a step or two down, adjust your safety strap and start on the next one. After about 10 steps or so and you had worked your way almost back down to the ground, you could then place the bottom (wooden) step. Or, you could place the three detachable steps. The detachable ones were generally preferred because they were best at preventing kids from trying to climb the pole. Anyway, as can be seen, stepping a pole was no easy task, but all in a day's work!

Another "All in a day's work" job consisted of checking our ladders for possible dry-rot. Recall they were made of wood and therefore subject to rot and deterioration with age. Somewhere in each work center was a large, heavy concrete weight with a chain and hook on each end. We had to get our ladder off our truck, place it horizontally on saw-horses or barrels, and systematically place the weight on each rung of the ladder. Then, with weight attached, we took our lineman's hammer and pounded on the rung. Theoretically, if there was rot in the rung that was not evident with visual inspection, the weight and pounding would cause it to break. This type of inspection and test was done periodically and with due seriousness. Falling from a ladder due to a rotten rung was the last thing anyone wanted to do. And, it was not anything the Company wanted to explain to a distressed spouse and/or to a newspaper reporter.

Are there any free services like pre-wiring any longer? I don't think so! Any new house or apartment building that went up got pre-wired. It was just one more FREE service provided by the good old

Bell System Companies (as I once again take up my soapbox). Anyway, we had so much new growth in the Cape Area that we were busy as bee's just working orders for new service. We didn't have time for pre-wiring during regular hours. So, after our orders were worked for the day, we traveled to a new apartment building and did pre-wiring. Many days, we didn't finish our regular orders until 7 or 8 o'clock. That meant we worked until midnight on pre-wires. The money was great, but it got old pretty fast. Our wives, however, had no trouble shopping all day and spending all that overtime money!

Recall how everything was measured in terms of per million man hours worked. The Bell System monitored just about every phase of the job using that form of measurement. If one particular measurement got out of hand a meeting would be called to discuss how to fix it. Often, there would be film to explain what was going wrong and how to fix it. Accidents of all types were also included in that type of measurement. With so many rookies on the job, it is a wonder there weren't more accidents. For example, I had a trouble report way out in the country. Upon arriving at the location, the trouble was obvious. The customer was served by Multiple Rural Wire. Remember that stuff? It consisted of a bunch of multi-colored, paired wires wound around a central large gauge wire. It was placed as a temporary expedient instead of cable. It was never meant to last for long, but as one might expect, it was never replaced until it began causing too much trouble. Anyway, my trouble was obvious....the wire had been shot by a hunter or a troublemaker. About half of the wires were dangling down from the point of the shot. Naturally, it was about 25 feet out from the pole. Since the location was very rural, the spans from pole to pole were much longer than normal. In my instance, they were at least 400 foot spans.

Well, my rookie solution to the problem was to climb the pole, loosen the attachment at the "J" Hook and lower the wire to the ground. I would then make the repairs and raise the wire back up. Good Heavens! What a stupid thing to do! Those 400 foot spans on each side of the pole only weighed about 300 pounds. When I loosened the attachment, the Rural Wire fell down across my safety belt and pinned me right to the pole. My hooks dug into the pole from all the extra weight that I couldn't move a muscle. I was way out in the country and miles from any help.

Almost frantically, I clipped into the wire and called my foreman for help. He was an old timer and knew outside plant as well as anyone. He listened to my situation and calmly told me what I should do. Knowing my young age and youthful body strength, he told me that I could indeed lift that wire off my safety belt and back onto the J Hook. It was so heavy; I just didn't know I could do that. For all I knew, it weighed a thousand pounds. Thank goodness, he was right! I put the old muscle to it and lifted it back up on the "J" Hook. He told me not to worry about the repair, just get off the pole and come on back to the work center. After that ordeal, my leg muscles were so rubbery that I almost never got my hooks out of that pole. Coming down the pole was even worse as I could hardly feel my legs and hooks as they hit the pole. Once down, I thanked my lucky stars, my foreman and the Good Lord! Another rookie lesson learned the hard way, but solidly logged in the book of experience!

Safety was a big part of the job! There were weekly meetings on safe driving as well as a hundred other subjects. Another test had to do with checking our hooks for sharpness and contour. We had a small metal gauge which would effectively measure the sharpness of the spike as well as the proper shape required to enter the pole and hold without cutting back out. Both sharpness and contour was adjusted with a simple flat file....a most useful tool found in every installer's tool box.

While on the subject of the flat file, recall its use on screwdrivers and drill bits. The days of throw-away everything had not yet arrived. When our screwdrivers became a little used or rounded off, we got out our file and sharpened them back into shape. It was the same with drill bits. These days, there are clever little devices to automatically sharpen bits. I don't like them! Give me that old flat file any day!

<"You'd never guess he splices telephone wire for a living! Heaven help us!"

CHAPTER 19 - THE TELEPHONE PIONEERS

It was my good fortune and pleasure to serve as President of my Telephone Pioneer Chapter, one of the most rewarding and worthwhile things I have ever done. For many years, the Telephone Pioneers was the largest industrial, volunteer community service organization and the absolute envy in the national business community. The key to success was in the basic organization, i.e. each chapter decided its own projects. This concept even reached down to the individual member. If a member had a worthwhile project and presented it to the chapter for adoption, chances were good it would be taken on. There was always something for everyone to get behind, something that would spark their interests, and involve each individual member. There was very little Company intervention. Pioneering always had the "clout" of the Company, which got their foot in almost any door, but they were generally left alone to do their own thing. All of this led to a feeling by the members of doing something worthwhile on their own for the community and for the Company outside the direct supervision of their Company bosses.

Unfortunately, in the last few years, Pioneering has become a different type of organization. They are no longer called Telephone Pioneers or even Telecom Pioneers….just Pioneers….not associated with the old Companies, but rather a separate, stand-alone charity similar to United Way or the Salvation Army. And, they are on their own financially as well. AT&T Pioneers are still around, but with little to no support from the Company. Strangely, they still look to the Pioneers for company branding opportunities. Remnants of the old clubs and chapters are generally made up of retirees who are struggling to keep it going. It will be very difficult unless the AT&T Company offers more support (in my humble opinion).

The original three tenets of Fellowship, Loyalty and Service are no longer used. These days, it's all about community service. There are still many good and worthwhile community service projects undertaken and completed; but the downside, however, has been in the loss of volunteer participation. Often, the projects undertaken are those dictated by the Company and member participation is nowhere near what it used to be. Membership (consisting mainly of retirees) has declined steadily. Fellowship has always been a priority with retirees, but advanced age of those left is hindering participation. The other tenet of Loyalty….well, it died with "corporate down-sizing", "restructuring" and "branding". Little wonder!

The Telephone Pioneer Organization was founded back in 1911 with the tenets mentioned above. The founders decided that membership qualifications should be twenty-one years of service in the industry probably in keeping with the name "Pioneer". That requirement was reduced to zero over the course of several years during the Eighties.....one of the first stakes in the Pioneer heart (again, in my humble opinion). There were many more changes that came later, which transformed Pioneering into something far different than originally intended by the founders. By the way, doesn't that sound familiar? Isn't our country going through a similar transition? Heaven help us!

For years, Pioneering was important to the Companies, and they didn't mind spending a little money and giving people a little time off the job for volunteer projects. I'm sure it got expensive at times, but much of the costs came from chapter assemblies, regional meetings, etc. These events, although useful for organizational planning, always included invitations to many senior executives who had done very little for Pioneering. I'm not saying that was wrong, only that it added substantially to the overall cost of Pioneering to the Company. I don't think the senior executives ever extracted those costs from the total when assessing the "costs and value" of Pioneering. If they had done so, the company benefits from Pioneering would have been shown to be extremely inexpensive....and very worthwhile.

One of the nicest compliments about Pioneering came from a Pioneer Partner (spouse of a member). While attending a monthly chapter meeting and listening to the list of projects we had on our plate, she said, "You know, the Pioneers do more good work in the community than most churches." Well, Pioneering is a different kind of work than church work, but it was still a nice compliment.

An old "Pioneer" certificate

All of the above said, I have a prediction. One of these days, I think company executives will look back on the old Pioneer Organization and wonder why they ever allowed it to change.

Things done just for the sake of change often relate more to ego than real benefits. The old clique' "If it ain't broke, don't fix it" was ridiculed so severely that people stopped using it almost altogether. Change became the new buzz word….and still is, huh! I don't recall the Telephone Pioneer Organization being broken!

Let’s do a comparison study......

THE OLD "PIONEER PURPOSE"

To promote and provide a means of friendly association for the longer service employees in the telephone industry, both active and retired

To foster among them a continuing fellowship and a spirit of mutual helpfulness

To exemplify and perpetuate those principles which have come to be regarded as the ideals and traditions of our industry

To participate in activities that are of service to the community; contribute to the progress of the association and promote the happiness, well-being and usefulness of the membership.

THE NEW "MISSION STATEMENT"

Pioneering is a network of volunteers, who effect immediate change in local communities with its sponsors.

Well the changes are obvious, aren’t they?

Rest in peace, Ma Bell.

CHAPTER 20 – CONCLUSION

Things change, don't they? And, we all get older! The late and great comedian and actor, George Burns used to sing a song entitled, I wish I was 18 again. I can relate to that! I had such fun coming up in the good old telephone business and I, too, wish I could go back and do it all over again.

There were so many life changing experiences. Oh yes! You have had some similar ones............

• The small bakery where we stopped for coffee and sweet rolls until going there on a trouble and finding the place full of roaches

• The Puritan Hotel where the young, baby-faced telephone man got his first surprise greeting and hugs by the "ladies"

• Working on a pole when a car pulled up below and the young couple made love unaware of the kid on hooks up above

• The first "hit-on" experience by an attractive young housewife

• Work in the town hospital where modesty was of no concern, but shocking to a young telephone man

• First trouble report in the Psychiatric Ward

• Pay Station repair in the local college girls dormitory

• Working installation in the embalming room of the funeral home (weird tools hanging from the walls)

• Installing service for the local Gypsies while trying to keep an eye on truck and tools

• Walking up on a moonshine still while on toll line repair

• Freezing near to death working in a refrigerated warehouse

• Burning near to death working in a glass works factory

• Suffocating near to death working in a sheep tannery

• Starving near to death working extended hours of service restoration

• Wondering how to discreetly run "JK" over the fitting rooms in a women's dress shop

• Operator duty during a union strike

• Trying to stay friends with "craft" associates while on strike duty

• Working in a home brewery when it was raided by the sheriff

To the good folks who are still working in the business, I know things are not the same and that beautiful old "Bell System" magic is gone. But, there have been some improvements as well.....thanks to the good work you do. So hang in there until they make you an offer you can't refuse. And, while you're waiting, see if you can restore Customer Service! Good Grief! I hate listening to all those options and pushing one for English or another for whatever…and winding up nowhere!

Before ending, I want to throw one more thought out on the table for the retirees. Remember the great country music group, *Alabama*? They sang a song entitled 40 Hour Week. I'll paraphrase some of the lyrics as follows:

Hello American Workers let me thank you for your time.
You work a forty hour week for a living,
just to send it on down the line.

We all did that, didn't we! And, we fed our families, sent our kids to school and at the end we got our wristwatch! Somehow, it doesn't seem quite fair....it was not enough! People of Hollywood, of the Media, of Politics, or Sports regularly receive quite extravagant awards when they do something well....sometimes even when they haven't done so well. I'm not against due recognition, but in most cases they just did what they were being paid to do! What about all those who work their 40 hour week (an expression meaning a lifetime) just doing their job? There should be equal accolades for the telephone man or woman, the butcher, the plumber, the electrician, the beautician, the preacher, the miner, the truck driver, the cashier, the baker, and every other everyday worker! Why not? They work just as hard or harder. They're just as dedicated to their craft and they give up a large portion of their lives to provide their particular service. I think there should be an Oscar program for everyday workers and it should be televised all day long on Labor Day! I'll dream on a while with that one! But doesn't it just seem like the fair thing to do?

Recently, I listened to a cute little Olympian female athlete tell how she had worked so long and so hard to get there. I'm sure she was well qualified and I appreciate her ability, talent and dedication; however, she was only sixteen! Good grief! She has no idea of the kind of sacrifice it takes to stay on the job for 30, 35, 40 years in order to support a family!

Well, I'll make that my final soap box speech!

THE TELEPHONE MAN

Oh, it's 8 o'clock! I've got to get in gear!
Where are my orders? Do I have all my sets?
Oh, I've got to get out of here!

OK, I'm pulling out! Stop! Look both ways.
Now where was that first order?
Aw, did I turn the wrong way?

No, what am I thinking? That was right!
We always go for coffee first,
Down at the Donut Delite.

Oh, I hope Sam, Guy and Jimmy are there, I love the stories they tell. And they know more of them
Than Alexander Graham Bell.

What a fun job! Why I'd do it for free.
It's like I'm a kid again, climbing up a tree.

Just give me a Southern Pine Creosote, about a 40 foot Class 5. And let me look down on the whole world
And up at that big blue sky.

Let me see now, Can I still reach that Number 10 pin?
I mean, after all, I'm not as young as I was back then.

Humph! Not even close! Why I couldn't ever get up the pole. It's this old back, you know The years have taken a toll.

But I'd do it all over again, if only I could, because there were things left to do.

But only on one condition my friends,
Only if I could do it again with YOU!.......Judge

ABOUT THE AUTHOR

“Judge” Pattengill is proud to be "an old telephone man". He began his telephone career in the Plant Department with C&P (Chesapeake & Potomac Telephone Co.) in West Virginia. That was followed by several years with GTE (General Telephone of Florida). Southern Bell came next and retirement followed at Bellsouth Company Headquarters in Atlanta.

He is a graduate of Rollins College. He holds a private pilot license and a real estate license, but is most proud of his many years of volunteer work with the Telephone Pioneers of America. He was Chapter President of the old Dogwood Chapter in Atlanta. Retired for many years, he still enjoys writing, painting and talking with old telephone friends. He is proud to be a Master Mason.

His friends include many other old telephone men and women who in their own way contributed to this book. To name them all would surely lead to omissions and that would be regrettable; however, those of perhaps strongest influence are Tom Norman, Sam Templeton, Guy Hammond, Jimmy McMullen, Gene Thornton, George Trueworthy, W.C. Smith, Jere Randall, Betty Wright McCowan, Amber Jaynes, Sara Davis, Sandy Saxton, Bonnie Wagner, Robert Britton, Sue Wofford, Bill Meeks, Tommy Millirons, Tom Walden, Ike Byrd, Mario Soto, Len Webb, Wayne Ates, Warren Blanks, Hazel Right, Jean Belec, Bill Craft, Gordon Titus, Harold Orum, Ralph Nolan, Doris Knot, Bob Weir, Bob Ringstrand, Ed Honeycutt, Russell Paschal, Diane Reisert, Harry McElveen, Dick Snelling, Woodrow Smith, Bob Lynch, Frank Moncer, Charles Sosebee, Chuck Herndon and Don Wright.

WWI Army Signal Corps

Another branch of ***Just Old Telephone Men***

This photo is dedicated to my friend and boss, General Thomas H. Norman, Army Signal Corps WWII

CLOSING THOUGHTS & A FEW FRIENDS

The most satisfaction I had in writing *Just An Old Telephone Man – 1st Edition* was corresponding with the readers. I heard from people from all over the country plus Canada, Great Britain and Australia. Good Heavens! Who would have ever thought there would be that much interest; yet, in retrospect why not? We worked in a truly great business for some truly great companies. And, we shared interests with more fellow workers than probably any other business. We could have formed our own army with all the necessary skills and talents and capabilities to get even the biggest of jobs done. In fact, we did that very thing.....we built the largest and best telephone system in the world. And, we had fun doing it!

Listed here (in no particular order) are a few of the kind folk who bought the first book, expressed their feelings and gave me a lot of encouragement for a 2nd Edition.

Richard Yarbrough
It was fun reading and reminded me of things I had long forgotten – green trucks, the Three C's and left-in-stations."

Mike Dudash
"It's hard to believe how well I can relate to some of the stories."

Paul Glasso
"Please send me three more books for my friends."

Joe Leonburger
"Just a note of thanks for the books. I'm sending one on to a friend of mine in Maryland."

Dave Gruger
"I really enjoyed reading your book. We need to meet and swap stories."

Steve Etts
"I really enjoyed reading the book. It brought back fond memories."

Connie Rollins
"We both have enjoyed the book. Ken knew a couple of your friends you listed. It brought back a lot of good telephone times."

Tom Iverson
"A sincere thanks."

Bill Baird
A fellow pilot and telephone man

Kevin King
"The book got here last night. It exceeded my expectations. I could have passed out a case at work. I grew up in a small town near Yosemite National Park. We had Sierra Telco. I had the best party line in town, the owner of the newspaper and the town-gossip both on my line. I always wondered if the paper used that line as a source."

Outside Plant Magazine

PhoneCo, Inc

Diane Reisert
"I enjoyed reading your book. It brought back a lot of memories of my old operator days."

Dave Heimer
"Yo' Judge! Obviously, we share quite a few experiences."

Bill from Hershey
"As for chuckles, I didn't get the first one until I was all the way in to Chapter #1 (Coffee Breaks). As a new hire, I was placed with one of the old timers. It must have been a year later that I found out you don't get two coffee breaks in the morning and two more in the afternoon!"

Randy Pevec
"My father retired with 35 years service and I had 9 years myself. The Telephone Industry has had a profound impact on my life as I heard all the stories from the old timers throughout my life. I intend to donate your book to the local library in memory of my father."

Sandy Pilgrim
"Please send me the book. Thank you."

Clayton Brown
"I am enjoying the book. Time to head for the barn.....one of the things we would say at quitting time."

Carol Barthel
"My husband, Al, retired in 1994 due to a stroke. We heard about your book at a Telephone Pioneer meeting. Please send us a copy."

Robert Britton
"I received the books and my techs liked them starting with whatever page they turned to."

Tim Patterson
"I am sending the names of the 19 techs in my group. Also please send an extra one for my father, Pat Patterson."

Richard Smith – Future Voice Systems
"Thank you for writing this book. It has reminded me of my years with Mountain Bell and the Pioneers. I really liked my job."

Robbie Goodson
"Just wanted to let you know I received the books and I loved them. I can't wait to give a copy to my father-in-law and uncle. Every time my family gets together, they always end up talking about the telephone company. I'm sure you know how that is."

Wendell Olson
"Hi Judge. I really enjoyed the book. Terrific style of presenting some of the humor about the 'phone factory'. I always wanted to

compile some stories myself. I would have called it, 'The Phone's Dead! Call the Operator!'"

Sandy Cole
"As a former PBX Operator with countless encounters with telephone people, I can't explain how much your book meant to me. Thank you so much."

Linda Niedringhaus – Applewood Books
"We all perused your book and found those anecdotes VERY amusing. Thanks for giving us a great lift at the office and we wish you well."

Sonny Campbell
"Your book was a hoot! Thanks for sharing some of your stories, many I can relate to. Take care and watch those 3 C's."

Terry Ozment – AT&T Sales Manager
"Thank you for your book. My dad is retired from Northwestern Bell and he will love it."

Bud Jones
"I'll be showing the book to fifteen or so retired outside plant people who I have breakfast with and will take orders!"

Greg Tennyson
"If you were here in Milwaukee, I'd take you out for coffee!

Stan Hitchcock
"I received a copy of your book from Robert Britton, a GREAT boss! I enjoyed it very much. Thanks for the memories........."

Amber Jaynes – Athens Pioneer President
"Thanks so much for the book and for your offer of more copies to help with next year's fundraising."

Robin Pittman
"Hi Judge! Send me four more books for the other Network Techs here."

Hasn't this been fun! Thank you so much for your time and your presence as we have reminisced together some good "old telephone" experiences. I have thoroughly enjoyed your companionship and as we part, I wish you good health, happiness and enjoyment of life.

"*Judge*"

May your best foot be forward and your wallet be fat
May your laces stay tied and your tires not go flat
May your eyes have a twinkle and your step have a bounce
May you eat all you want and gain nary an ounce
May you always hang out with the friendliest folks
May they take your advice and laugh at your jokes
May you day be exempt from all hassle and sorrow
But not even half as much fun as tomorrow.

THE END

Made in the USA
Las Vegas, NV
17 September 2024